THE
MULTIPLICATION
CHALLENGE

A Strategy to Solve
Your Leadership Shortage

Steve Murrell exudes and models leadership. I've learned much from him, and you will too!

—ED STETZER
Billy Graham Distinguished Chair and Professor, Wheaton College
Executive Director, Billy Graham Center

I like to read leadership books by people who are leading, and that is why I highly recommend *The Multiplication Challenge* by Steve Murrell. Steve redefines leadership and brings it back to a biblical foundation for how leaders should think, act, grow, and multiply. Writing from his experience of leading Victory, which has grown to more than 85,000 Christ-followers, gives this book enough credibility that every leader should buy a copy!

—DAVE FERGUSON
Author of *Finding Your Way Back to God*
Lead Visionary for NewThing

Steve Murrell is an exceptional leader who demonstrates deep humility and a will to succeed. He has a rare combination of a strong mind and a resilient heart. Steve spent the past thirty years developing leaders in a nation once foreign to him, and these leaders have in turn continued to raise thousands across the globe. I am a grateful recipient of Steve's leadership. I believe this book provides a solution to transformational challenges for the future and is a profitable read for anyone in business and politics who purposes to leave a leadership legacy.

—RACHEL ONG
Founder and Chief Executive, ROHEI
Executive Producer, Cozeh

For over two decades now, Pastor Steve Murrell has quietly taught me significant lessons in leadership and in life. There are many principles we can learn from this book, but what really stood out for me is this: that "the heart of leadership is humility and service." Steve has lived it, mastered it, and shared it. I recommend this book as a must-read for everyone looking to inspire and empower others to lead.

—ERIC ALTAMIRANO
Head Basketball Coach, National University Bulldogs

There are dream leaders, theory leaders, and action leaders. Steve Murrell is an action leader with proven fruit of his leadership. He is a level-five leader in the church today. This book is pure gold, read and act upon it.

—FRANK DAMAZIO
Pastor, City Bible Church
Chairman, Ministers Fellowship International

Here is a gem on Christian leadership essentials from a servant-leader practitioner I admire. Victory has often been asked why it has so many strong leaders. Here's their big story with many little stories. I will keep coming back to this book as a resource for leadership training that's biblically grounded, inspiring, and practical.

—TIM D. GENER, PhD
President and Professor of Theology, Asian Theological Seminary

This is the book I've been waiting for Steve Murrell to write. My wife and I also served as church planters in Manila for eighteen years, so we watched firsthand the growth and expansion of Every Nation. Steve and his team are building big churches around the world because they're building big people. Big people know how to serve with courage, despite the circumstances and temptations. Steve and Deborah have modeled the way, and I'm delighted that they're now sharing it with all of us in print.

—DR. CHUCK QUINLEY
President, Emerge Missions

The Multiplication Challenge is a practical but biblical guide on servant leadership. From Nashville to Manila and other points of mission, Pastor Steve dramatically tells true stories demonstrating how a leader ought to think, act, listen, and relate. Shored up by apt quotations, he deftly weaves principle and practice to drive home the message that leadership is serving in humility, not in authoritarianism; setting an example, not sporting a title; training and equipping others to lead, not perpetuating one's self in power. Pastors, missionaries, church workers, officials, lay leaders, and those who believe that leadership should be tethered to selfless service will find this book basic yet exceptional.

—RUBEN T. REYES
Associate Justice of the Philippine Supreme Court (retired)
Vice President, Judicial Council, United Methodist Church

When Steve and Deborah started their work in the Philippines, our families were friends, and I watched with interest how Steve led with great vision and humility. Each time our families were together, I learned important leadership principles from him. Reading this book reminded me of those times together. This book is like sitting down and having a conversation about leadership with a man who speaks not only with expertise, but with a heart and passion to do God's work. It was a great privilege to watch him lead.

—EDDIE LYONS
Senior Pastor, High Street Baptist Church
President, Baptist Bible Fellowship International

Leadership is inherent in every single one of us. Beyond an ability to lead, it is a capacity to choose the right path, inspire passion, and solicit compassion. Pastor Steve will rouse the leader in you through this book. My own life is a testament to his exemplary leadership.

—ALFRED ROMUALDEZ
Mayor, City of Tacloban, Philippines

Steve powerfully tackles one of the biggest problems for churches in our time today—that of raising enough leaders who will faithfully take on the Great Commission. He is not just writing from theory, but from actual implementation of these principles. I strongly recommend that leaders read this book. May the insights and perspectives offered here awaken churches and renew in us a commitment to multiply—to make disciples who will make disciples for the glory of God.

—DR. PETER TAN-CHI
Senior Pastor, Christ's Commission Fellowship

Steve Murrell didn't just start a church, he started a movement. In this book, Steve shares how rapid growth exposed a leadership crisis, causing his church to radically reset their growth goals from 75,000 to 5,000. The way he unpacks practical leadership development and discipleship methods for future leaders makes this book a must-read!

—ROB HOSKINS
President, OneHope, Inc.
Board Chair, Oral Roberts University

Oftentimes, Christian leaders are so keen to make disciples, they forget a foundational component of the disciple-making process: first developing good leaders who are equipped to make good disciples. In *The Multiplication Challenge*, Steve Murrell shows how important intentional leadership development is to the making of disciples, as well as to the growth of churches and ministries. *The Multiplication Challenge* gives us the tools to develop a leadership culture, the essentials of the leadership-development process, and guidelines for leaving a leadership legacy. All those involved in the Great Commission—a task of making disciples of all the people groups of our world—need to read this book!

—LARRY W. CALDWELL, PhD
Academic Dean, Sioux Falls Seminary
Director of Training and Strategy, Converge Worldwide

THE
MULTIPLICATION CHALLENGE

A Strategy to Solve
Your Leadership Shortage

STEVE MURRELL & WILLIAM MURRELL

CREATION
HOUSE

DEDICATION
To the unknown, unrecognized, under-honored leaders
who quietly build men and women, rather than monuments

Published by Creation House
A Charisma Media Company
600 Rinehart Rd., Lake Mary Florida 32746
creationhouse.com

Trade Paperback ISBN: 978-1-62998-574-9
E-book ISBN: 978-1-62998-575-6
Library of Congress Control Number: 2016953795

First Edition

16 17 18 19 20 21 - 5 4 3 2 1

Printed In Canada

CONTENTS

FOREWORD

Steve Murrell gets it. Under his leadership, Victory Manila grew from a small church of less than 200 people into a mammoth ministry that reaches over 85,000. He's not a discipleship theorist. He's a world-class practitioner.

But it's not just the incredible growth that sets Steve and Victory Manila apart. It's the way they've grown. They've done it the old-fashioned way—or better yet, the biblical way—by making disciples who actually make disciples. What a novel idea!

I first learned about this amazing ministry when the leadership team from one of their larger campuses came to North Coast Church to learn how we do small groups. Five minutes into our initial conversation, I was dumbfounded. Why had *they* flown halfway around the world to learn from *me*?

It made no sense.

Their ministry was nearly six times larger than ours. They were multiplying disciples at an exponential rate. But there they were, pen in hand, taking copious notes while I tried to act and sound insightful.

Yet it's precisely this humble spirit that sets Steve (and the rest of the Victory Manila team) apart. They don't rest on their laurels. They're willing to go anywhere to learn from anyone if it will help them do a better job of making disciples.

I've been a big fan ever since.

When I found out that Steve was writing a book on developing and multiplying leaders, I knew I had to read it. When he asked me to write the foreword, I knew it was the best way to get an early look at what promised to be a great manuscript. I was right.

It took just a few pages for me to realize that Steve has grasped something that most passionate church leaders miss: *the subtle (but incredibly important) difference between making disciples and raising up leaders.*

We multiply disciples by teaching them to walk on an increasing path of obedience. We develop and multiply leaders by teaching them to walk on an increasing path of servanthood. The two are closely related. But they are different.

Jesus had many disciples. He had a much smaller group of intentionally and strategically trained leaders.

A healthy church follows His example. Like a train, it runs on two rails. One is discipleship. The other is developing and multiplying leaders. Neglect either one, and the train will tip over.

Ministries that try to turn every disciple into a leader end up with lots of exhausted and discouraged saints trying to become what they were never cut out to be. Ministries that neglect developing and multiplying leaders eventually stall out as their leaders become overwhelmed and ineffective.

In *The Multiplication Challenge,* Steve takes us on a journey that starts with his own shocking realization that despite the impressive and much ballyhooed growth of Victory Manila, the train was about to tip over.

Foreword

As you read these pages, you'll discover how biblical leaders think, and how they're identified, trained, and released to serve rather than be served.

It's a book that just might keep your ministry from tipping over.

—LARRY OSBORNE
Pastor and Author
North Coast Church, Vista, California
2016

PREFACE

On March 28, 1990, the Chicago Bulls beat the Cleveland Cavaliers in an overtime thriller that would prove to be one of Michael Jordan's greatest games.

When Bulls' rookie forward Stacey King was asked about the historic game, he commented (humorously), "I'll always remember this as the night that Michael Jordan and I combined to score 70 points." The box score from that night read like this: "M. Jordan: 69 points [18 rebounds, and 6 assists]. S. King: 1 point [1 rebound, and 1 assist]."

As coauthor of this book on leadership, I feel a little bit like Stacey King. I'll always remember this as the time that my dad and I wrote a leadership book. Here's how it happened.

Between stints in graduate school, I spent a wonderful year working for my dad at Every Nation's Nashville office in Tennessee. Most of my daily work was administrative, but on some days, I found myself a scribe in meetings that were way over my pay grade—meetings where important topics were discussed and big decisions were made.

In one such meeting, my dad was discussing a promotion plan for his (then) newly released book called *WikiChurch*. After a plan was hatched and to-dos were assigned, the conversation turned to the possibility of a follow-up book. What would my dad write and publish next?

The group consensus was that the next book should be about leadership. If *WikiChurch* told the story of Victory Manila's discipleship culture, then the next book would tell the story of Victory Manila's leadership culture.

After that discussion, nothing happened for several months, but when I approached my final few months of working at Every Nation (before heading off to graduate school), I asked my dad if he would like for me to do some initial research for the leadership book. My research included digging through a decade of my dad's blogs and sermons for content and stories that might be worth including in such a book. It also included interviewing pastors and leaders from Victory Manila about their experiences working with my dad during his thirty years as a pastor in the Philippines.

Between the fascinating interviews and the scores of leadership blogs my dad had written over the years, I found myself with lots of material on hand. Eagerly putting my historian skills to use, I began analyzing and organizing the material. I drafted a book outline and chapter outlines. I organized old blog posts and leadership stories based on where they might fit best in the book. It was all an attempt to make my dad's actual writing process as straightforward as possible. But at my dad's prompting, I myself began turning some of those chapter outlines into written content—sometimes reworking principles from an old blog and other times, retelling stories from the interviews that I had conducted in Manila.

On my last day at Every Nation, I placed a large file folder on my dad's desk entitled, "Leadership Book Project." The file included rough drafts of about half of the chapters, with outlines and extensive notes for the remaining chapters.

That was August 2012.

Since then, my dad has written two other books, *100 Years from Now* (2013) and *My First, Second & Third Attempts at Parenting* (2015), and I have written two dissertation chapters. For several years, I assumed that the leadership book project was dead, but last fall, my dad asked me to dig up my old files. Over the last few months, he has been feverishly writing the remaining chapters from the original outline, rewriting some of my chapters, and even adding new chapters to the book.

Once the book was completed, I found out through a friend in Every Nation's Communications Department that my dad intended to list me as coauthor on the book. I was shocked. I assumed that he would give me a shout-out in the introduction for doing a little research and ghostwriting some of the project, but I never imagined that the first book with my name on the front cover would be a book about leadership (and not history).

At first, I argued strongly not to list me as a coauthor.

My name added no value to the book. If I was a young pastor or campus missionary, I argued, it would make sense to include me. Or perhaps if I was the founder and owner of a successful business (like my brothers), it might make sense to include me. But I'm an academic—a member of a guild of solo-acts who hate leading and hate being led. Furthermore, I have almost zero leadership experience.

Besides a rather forgettable stint on my eighth grade student council, the largest thing I've led in my life is a small group Bible study. So though I did spend several months researching and interviewing for this book, and though I ghostwrote some of the chapters, this is definitely a Michael Jordan and Stacey King-type partnership. The book is based on my dad's leadership experiences in his many decades as a church planter, cross-cultural missionary, and cofounder of a global church-planting movement. This is his book.

For weeks, I protested the coauthorship idea. But then it hit me—what my dad was doing in making me coauthor was exactly what he had been doing for over thirty years of ministry.

I began to recall story after story from my interviews with leaders in Manila of my dad taking inexperienced emerging leaders and inviting them to lead with him. In the early days (so my sources tell me), he did most of the work and gave them much of the credit. Why? Because what mattered to him was that he and the emerging leader were leading together. Over time, those emerging leaders became experienced and established leaders. And not only did they take on more leadership responsibility, but they also began raising up leaders to lead alongside them.

That's the story of this book—and the story of how my name got on it.

Enjoy.

—WILLIAM S. MURRELL, JR.

INTRODUCTION

WHEN 5,000 IS GREATER THAN 75,000

September 2009. Two dozen key leaders from our church, Victory Manila, were having an off-site strategy meeting to plan for the next decade. As we looked at the five-digit number on the whiteboard, most of the leaders in the room seemed to accept our new faith goal with a sense of excitement.

75,000.

Even though a month had passed, we were still riding the wave of momentum created by our church's twenty-fifth anniversary event. Just four weeks prior, we had been face-to-face with over 30,000 Filipinos at the celebration. Today, we were face-to-face with a huge number on a whiteboard.

75,000.

Victory Manila's anniversary celebration was held at the Smart Araneta Coliseum, a.k.a. the "Big Dome," which was the largest indoor arena in the Philippines at the time. (Araneta was also the site of the famous Ali-Frazier boxing match in 1975—the "Thrilla in Manila.") So many people registered for the anniversary event, we had to run two back-to-back services in the 16,000-seat arena.

The anniversary celebration in the Big Dome was all about looking back at the past twenty-five years. Our strategic meeting in that small conference room was all about looking ahead and dreaming for the next twenty-five years. Specifically, we wanted to upgrade our discipleship process for Victory Manila—to figure out how to more effectively *engage* our culture and community, *establish* biblical foundations, *equip* believers to minister, and *empower* disciples to make disciples. (We call it the Four Es.)

At the time, more than 37,000 people were attending our weekend worship services across thirteen Metro Manila locations. Now we were looking ahead—to the number on the board.

75,000.

While everyone seemed excited about those five digits, I was not. As I looked at all those zeros, something felt wrong. I wasn't sure exactly what was wrong, but something was definitely wrong.

I don't really set goals, and my leadership style has always reflected this fact. In the first twenty-five years of Victory Manila, we had never set a numerical growth goal. Not even once. And strangely enough, we had never had a year when we didn't experience numerical growth. We had experienced twenty-five consecutive years of numerical growth, but had no growth goals.

After living and pastoring in Manila for over two decades, my role in Every Nation (our global movement) had changed, and I had begun splitting time between Manila, Nashville, and Every Nation churches around the world. In my absence, the Manila leadership team had decided to try some faith goals, and I tried to go along with it. I had equipped and empowered my team to lead, and now they were leading. But something still seemed wrong with this faith goal.

Finally, it hit me. The problem wasn't that we had a goal. I could live with a goal even if it wasn't my natural inclination. The problem was that number: 75,000. But why was it problematic? Was it too small? I have often had to repent for thinking too small. Maybe God expected us to think bigger.

CELEBRATING THE WRONG NUMBERS

Seventy-five thousand wasn't the only number that we looked at that day. Our team had prepared statistics on every aspect of our Metro Manila church—number of locations, number of services, total attendance, financial giving, baptisms, small groups, pastor-to-member ratio, youth service attendance, children's ministry volunteers, scholarship programs, and more.

As we examined our numbers, all of which seemed to be growing, my eyes fell on one set of numbers that had flatlined over the last four years (and was even showing hints of decline).

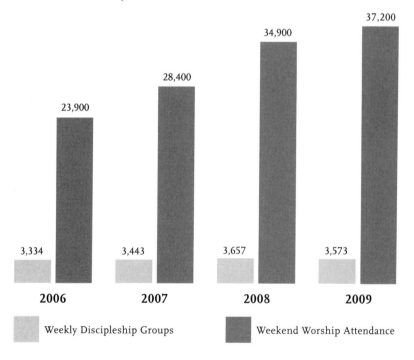

3,334	3,443	3,657	3,573
2006	**2007**	**2008**	**2009**

Weekly Discipleship Groups   Weekend Worship Attendance

As you can see on the chart, from 2006 to 2009, our Metro Manila church attendance had grown from 23,900 to 37,200. We had added over 13,000 people, but we had only started 239 new discipleship groups.

Eventually, our group discussion shifted from how to grow to 75,000 people to why we only had 3,573 small groups. Why were we growing explosively in weekend worship attendance, but decreasing in weekly discipleship groups? We were not only failing to equip and empower more disciples to make disciples, but we were also losing some of the people who had already been equipped.

As we looked at this seemingly isolated leadership void, we suddenly began to see leadership shortages everywhere—worship, preaching, children's ministry, administration, and technology, to name just a few. Our church had grown considerably over the last few years, and just about every department was feeling the growing pains. Our leaders, whether paid staff or key volunteers, were stretched thin, and we didn't have any reinforcements in sight.

The realization of our leadership shortage came quickly and erased all the enthusiasm that had carried over from our celebration the month before. That September, we realized that our growth had drastically outpaced our leadership development. We were quickly multiplying disciples, but only slowly adding leaders. We were in trouble, and suddenly, we knew it.

IT'S NOT JUST ABOUT MAKING DISCIPLES

A few years ago, I wrote a book about small-group discipleship that was based on my experience as a clueless missionary and church planter in Manila. The book was originally titled *Accidental Missionary*. My American publisher changed the name to *WikiChurch*.

If *WikiChurch* told the story of how Victory Manila grew from 165 to 52,000 people, then this book tells the story of how Victory Manila "shrank" from a goal of 75,000 to a goal of 5,000 (or simply, how we rediscovered the importance of leadership development).

WikiChurch began with a story about the twenty-fifth anniversary of Victory Manila, the church my wife and I helped start in 1984. That evening, as I looked out at the crowded arena, I asked myself, "Who are all these people and where did they come from?" In the book, I then proceeded to look back and tell the Victory story—where we started, who we started with, and how we gradually grew from a group of 165 college students to a church of 52,000 (in 2011, when *WikiChurch* was written). We grew because we mastered the "same ole boring strokes"—our Four Es—of discipleship.

A WikiChurch is a church that, like Wikipedia, empowers volunteers to contribute and participate in the mission of the organization. Wikipedia's mission is the rapid and widespread dissemination of encyclopedic information. In the case of a WikiChurch, the mission is the rapid and widespread dissemination of the gospel. This goal can only be achieved when non-professional Christians (electricians, lawyers, students, etc.) are equipped and empowered by the professionals (apostles, prophets, evangelists, pastors, teachers) to make disciples.

As obsessively focused as we were on making disciples, for a brief season, we forgot that we also needed to develop leaders. Accidentally and gradually, we became less intentional about identifying potential leaders, developing current leaders, and multiplying future leaders. This oversight resulted in a leadership crisis that threatened to derail everything we had worked so hard to create for over two decades.

It's very possible and very common to make disciples and not train leaders. A church can be effective in *engaging* culture and community, *establishing* biblical foundations, *equipping* believers to minister, and *empowering* disciples to make disciples—and still be reluctant or negligent in identifying, developing, and multiplying leaders.

That's the multiplication challenge.

Why?

Because there's a difference between empowering people to make disciples and trusting people to lead. If we want to have healthy churches, we need to do both. And we need to do both well.

I'm not suggesting that everyone is called to a leadership position in the church. And even people who are called to leadership positions have different levels of talents and gifts, as Jesus indicated in the Parable of the Talents. (See Matthew 25.)

THE PROBLEM WITH RAPID GROWTH

I do believe that every church and every campus ministry can and should grow stronger, larger, and more influential. If we are faithful in making disciples, Jesus will build His church. There are many reasons churches don't grow. Believe it or not, one reason some don't grow is that they don't really want to grow—because they know that growth causes problems.

The church in Jerusalem grew very rapidly after Jesus' ascension and quickly began to experience the problems that come with church growth. Here's a quick summary of their growth from the first few chapters of the book of Acts:

"In those days Peter stood up among the brothers (the company of persons was in all about *120*) . . ." (Acts 1:15).

"So those who received his word were baptized, and there were added that day about *three thousand* souls" (Acts 2:41).

". . . And the Lord *added to their number day by day* those who were being saved" (Acts 2:47).

"But many of those who had heard the word believed, and the number of the men *came to about five thousand*" (Acts 4:4).

"And *more than ever believers* were added to the Lord, *multitudes of both men and women* . . ." (Acts 5:14).

In these few verses, we see a church that grew from 120 scared believers to more than 5,000 in just a few months. However, while the growth was good, problems soon arose.

> Now in these days when the disciples were increasing in number, a complaint by the Hellenists arose against the Hebrews because their widows were being neglected in the daily distribution. And the twelve summoned the full number of the disciples and said, "It is not right that we should give up preaching the word of God to serve tables. Therefore, brothers, pick out from among you seven men of good repute, full of the Spirit and of wisdom, whom we will appoint to this duty. But we will devote ourselves to prayer and to the ministry of the word." (Acts 6:1-4)

Growing pains look different in different church contexts, but for the church in first-century Jerusalem, the problem was that the Hellenistic (or Greek) widows in the church were being overlooked in the daily food distribution—or that was the complaint. This oversight may have been early signs of ethnic and cultural division within the church in Jerusalem, or it may have been an indication of an administrative leadership void within the early church. I think it was probably both, but for the purposes of this discussion, we'll focus on the latter.

In this moment, Peter and the apostles realized that the church had grown too large for the twelve to lead effectively. Their leadership team of twelve had worked well with 120 believers, but not so well with over 5,000. What did they do? They chose seven capable men and turned responsibility over to them. This decision accomplished three things:

1. It solved the problem that some widows were being overlooked in the food distribution.
2. It empowered young and new leaders, including Stephen, who not long after this would become the first martyr of the early church.
3. It allowed the apostles to focus their attention on prayer and the ministry of the Word.

The result? More growth. "And the word of God continued to increase, and the number of the disciples multiplied greatly in Jerusalem, and a great many of the priests became obedient to the faith" (Acts 6:7).

God causes growth, and growth causes problems. But that doesn't mean that growth is itself a problem. Since God makes things grow, we should always pray for, expect, and celebrate growth. However, we should know that growth often exposes—and sometimes creates—leadership voids. If we don't respond wisely and quickly, people will be overlooked and leaders will be overwhelmed.

If we respond with urgency and wisdom, like the early church, then the Word of God will spread, and we will grow even more.

ARE YOU PLAYING THE NUMBERS GAME?

Like the church in Jerusalem, our church in Manila had experienced rapid growth—and the growth was about to sink us.

A couple of decades ago when I was a new church planter, I didn't have a clue what I was doing. But I didn't let that stop me. In those days, church growth was all the rage. I read books on church growth and took a pilgrimage to South Korea to visit the world's largest church, all in an attempt to learn how to grow a church. My primary motivation was a love for the lost, but it was probably also mixed with a bit of self-absorbed insecurity and youthful arrogance.

Early on, I had this idea that as long as there was one lost person in my city, then my church wasn't big enough. I still think that way, and I hope I never get over my obsessive-compulsive compassion for the lost.

While church-growth books and seminars seem to now be out of style in most Western church circles, I remain convinced that un-churched, de-churched, and anti-church people still matter to God, and they should matter to us. I'm convinced that we're supposed to do our best to engage our communities with the gospel. If we do a decent job at that, then our churches will grow.

Whether our growth is organic, organized, or orchestrated, growth will force us to deal with numbers. The trick is to figure out which numbers really matter and which ones don't.

Many church leaders make the mistake of thinking that the two most important numbers are tithes and Sunday attendance. However, those two numbers often deceive pastors, especially when they're on the increase.

In 2009, if we had focused on tithes and Sunday attendance in our September strategic planning meeting, we would have been deceived into thinking that we were doing great—better than ever, in fact. However, the reality was this: while our offerings and attendance numbers were up, and we were effectively engaging our communities and making disciples, we were not training nearly enough leaders.

SETTING THE RIGHT TARGET

Back to our strategic planning meeting.

As our meeting progressed, I eventually figured out why I was so troubled by the number written on our board. It was not too small. It was too big. Way too big.

So I walked to the board, erased it, and paused a moment before replacing it with a four-digit number. Having made peace for the first time in my life with goal setting, I boldly scribbled our new faith goal on the board.

5,000.

Reaching 75,000 in weekend attendance didn't matter. Our goal was to train new small-group leaders. At that time, we had roughly 3,500 small-group leaders. Our new goal was 5,000.

Everyone in the room immediately understood the significance of our new number. It represented discipleship rather than attendance. We all realized that we could have eventually reached 75,000 without focusing on discipleship but, in the process, we would cease to be the church God had called us to be. You can grow a church in many ways, but many of those ways have nothing to do with making disciples. Victory Manila exists to "honor God and make disciples." If we had set 75,000 as our faith goal, for the first time in our history, we would have been focusing on how many attended our church services rather than how many people were making disciples.

Our new number—5,000—refocused us on equipping and empowering people to make disciples. We have always believed that our job is to make disciples, not to build the church. Jesus said He would build His church. We make disciples; He builds His church. It's that simple.

Looking at those four digits, we all knew we had work to do. That day, we realized that if we were going to be serious and intentional about making disciples, we also needed to be serious and intentional about training small-group leaders.

This book tells the story of how we rediscovered the importance of intentional leadership development and how our growth goal went from 75,000 to 5,000.

THE MULTIPLICATION CHALLENGE

When a church or ministry experiences multiplication-type growth, but only develops leaders by addition, a serious leadership shortage results. That's the multiplication challenge: how to multiply leaders at a rate that keeps pace with growth. If you're experiencing exponential growth, the only way to keep up is by multiplying leaders.

This book is divided into three sections. "Creating a Leadership Culture" (chapters 1 through 5) focuses on how to develop a healthy leadership culture by thinking, acting, listening, growing, and multiplying like a leader.

"Discovering a Leadership Strategy" (chapters 6 through 9) explains how to develop leaders and how to apply the four leadership multipliers of our leadership-development strategy: *identification, instruction, impartation,* and *internship.*

"Leaving a Leadership Legacy" (chapters 10 through 13) discusses how to leave a leadership legacy through biblical ethics, multi-generational partnerships, systematic leadership development, and intentional empowerment of new leaders.

My prayer is that the principles and stories in these pages will help you address your multiplication challenge and solve your leadership shortage by teaching you to identify potential leaders, develop current leaders, and multiply future leaders in your church, campus ministry, or organization.

Seven years have passed since I erased 75,000 on that whiteboard and replaced it with 5,000. During those years, our Victory Manila small-group leaders have grown from 3,500 to over 10,000 small-group leaders and interns, and our worship attendance has grown from 37,000 to over 85,000. We continue to be obsessively focused on making disciples, and we are more intentional than ever about developing and multiplying leaders.

CREATING A
LEADERSHIP
CULTURE

1

HOW TO THINK LIKE A LEADER

He who is not a good servant will not be a good master.

PLATO, Philosopher

Being a public servant is a serious job, not like a boxer where you're entertaining people.

MANNY PACQUIAO, Senator/Boxer

"For even the Son of Man came not to be served but to serve, and to give his life as a ransom for many."

MARK 10:45

I was covered from head to toe with sweat, dust, and mud, but that didn't stop him. With flowing tears and quivering lips, he wrapped his arms around my filthy Tyvek protective suit and gave me the tightest hug of my life.

Then he took one step back, looked me in the eye and said, "Thank you. I can't believe a pastor is doing this for me and my wife." He repeated the tight muddy hug and said, "I've never seen a pastor do this."

What I couldn't believe was that this long-time church attendee was so surprised to see a pastor acting like a Christian. And I certainly wasn't the only pastor involved. In fact, almost everyone who works at Every Nation's Nashville office was doing exactly what I was doing.

Here's the context of those muddy hugs.

SAD WORDS I'LL NEVER FORGET

During the first weekend of May in 2010, parts of the United States—Middle Tennessee, Western Kentucky, and Northern Mississippi—were pummeled by torrential rainfall. The swelling rivers caused what was described as a "once-in-a-thousand-year flood" in Nashville.

The Cumberland River, which flows through the center of Nashville, has a flood stage of forty feet. After thirty-six hours of relentless rainfall, the Cumberland reached a record-breaking fifty-one feet and promptly filled the city with murky water. By the time the rain stopped, it had caused over two billion dollars in private home damage and over 120 million dollars in public infrastructure damage. Commercial damage included the famous Opry Mills Mall, which was filled with over ten feet of water in its 1.2 million square feet of retail and entertainment space. The reopening of Opry Mills required two years and over 200 million dollars in repairs.

I'll never forget the first day I volunteered with my three sons to help clean up some of the homes that had been destroyed. More than one hundred volunteers from area churches met at Bethel World Outreach Church (our Every Nation church in Nashville) early on a Saturday morning. A veteran Samaritan's Purse staff member gave us thirty minutes of training, organized us into groups of ten, led us in prayer, then sent us off to an address that represented a flooded home and a family that needed help.

My team was assigned to a lower income neighborhood south of Nashville. As we turned onto the street, I was stunned by the scene. The homes at the top of the hill escaped total destruction, but as we descended the hill toward our assigned address, I felt like we were driving into a war zone. It was a depressing picture of devastation and loss.

When we finally found our assigned address, we introduced ourselves to the homeowners. They both spoke excellent English, but with an accent that hinted that they were from West Africa, maybe Nigeria.

A week after the flood, the man and his wife were obviously still in shock. The wife thanked us for coming to help, while her husband repeatedly mumbled that he had lost everything. He sadly pointed to a huge pile of trash in his front yard and said, "That represents thirty years of hard work and savings. That's all I have. And look at it now. Trash."

The pile of wet and muddy trash included a television, a refrigerator, a microwave, beds, chairs, books, clothing, and other items that were so mud-covered, I couldn't even guess what they once were.

As we went to work pulling out muddy carpet and moldy insulation, I noticed that the homeowner was looking at me. I kept getting this feeling he was watching me. It happened several times during the first hour.

Finally, he approached me with a smile on his face. Pointing at me, he said enthusiastically, "I know who you are! You're that missionary pastor from Manila who preached at Bethel!"

"Yes, that's me. Are you a Bethel member?"

"No, but my wife and I visited a few times and heard you preach."

Then came the first hug. An hour later, he gave me the second hug.

At the end of our brief lunch break, he approached me a third time, hugged me again, and said, "Thank you, pastor! I can't believe this. I mean, I never imagined a pastor would get dirty and muddy cleaning my house. Why would a pastor do this?"

I said something about Jesus coming to serve, and that all Christians, especially pastors, are supposed to follow His example and serve.

His response was almost as sad as the destruction all around me. His words are still permanently burned in my brain. "In my country, we are taught to serve our pastors. Our pastors don't serve us."

Unfortunately, the idea of pastors expecting to be served, while not setting an example of service themselves, is not unique to West Africa. It's universal, and it seems to be increasing as more and more church leaders embrace a false gospel of entitlement.

As we will see in the coming pages, Jesus talked little about leading and much about serving. He was always more concerned with the heart than the actions—with how we think than what we do.

If we want to think like leaders, then we need to examine how Jesus led and study what He taught His leaders. But before we do that, let's properly define leadership.

WHAT IS LEADERSHIP?

This book was written to help you identify potential leaders, develop current leaders, and multiply future leaders.

Why? Because our understanding or misunderstanding of leadership will determine what kind of leaders (or non-leaders) we identify, develop, and multiply.

Complete this sentence: *Leadership is* _____ .

What word did you put in the blank? Influence? Power? Responsibility? Authority? Position? Title? Entitlement?

I imagine that unless we're all reading the same leadership book at the same time, this fill-in-the-blank statement will yield a number of different responses—some helpful and others not so helpful; some accurate and others flawed.

I have read many of the classic leadership books written in the past few decades by both Christian and non-Christian authors. While I have learned a great deal from these books, sometimes I think that leaders can become preoccupied with the idea of leadership and completely miss the basic point.

Leadership can be described and defined in so many valid ways. However, this book will focus on one description and one definition.

Leadership is *serving*. Therefore, to think like a leader means to think like a *servant*.

While this idea of serving doesn't necessarily negate other definitions of leadership, I do think it captures the heart of true leadership—at least the kind of leadership I want to identify, develop, and multiply. Defining leadership as serving is even more fundamental than the popular and helpful mantra: "Leadership is influence."

The "leadership is influence" idea is perhaps an accurate technical understanding of the social dynamic of leadership.

However, I would still argue that serving should precede influence in a biblical understanding of leadership. Why? Because Jesus seemed to teach influence not as an end but rather as a means—a means to serve. If we want to use both definitions together, maybe we could say that influence is the *what* of leadership and service is the *why* of leadership.

Think about it. What is the point of becoming a leader? Why do you want to be a leader?

If the desire to lead doesn't spring from a heart to serve, then we've completely missed the point of true leadership. Sure, we can read books, listen to podcasts, and apply the latest techniques to gain influence and authority. But if serving is not the end, then we aren't leading like Jesus.

CELEBRITY PASTORS, BODYGUARDS, AND BARISTAS

At a recent pastors' gathering, I watched in dismay as a celebrity pastor and his entourage filed out of a four-door Porsche that was parked in a heavily-guarded VIP parking section. The pastor and his crew strutted into the meeting like they were walking the red carpet at the Grammys. Later, as expected, their exit was as grand as their entrance. While I'm certain that there are aspects of my Western lifestyle that confuse people in developing nations, I must confess that I was embarrassed by the show put on by this pastor, his Porsche, and his entourage that included multiple bodyguards and armor-bearers.

On the other side of the world, I recently ministered in a nation that is actually dangerous for pastors. One brave pastor rolled up his pant leg to show me the bullet wound that he got when a radical Muslim fringe group attacked his church. Another pastor in that nation told me about an assassination attempt on his life. Fully armed men wearing ski masks entered his home to kill him. Fortunately, he had well-trained bodyguards who defended his family. Many Every Nation pastors live and minister in dangerous nations and need bodyguards. If someone is trying to kill you, then get a bodyguard. But please don't get a security team because you don't like to be around people. Pastors who don't like to be around people should consider another line of work.

In contrast to VIP parking and bodyguards, Jesus taught a more simple and humble leadership style. After thinking like a servant and washing His disciples' feet, He said, "'For I have given you an example, that you also should do just as I have done to you. Truly, truly, I say to you, a servant is not greater than his master, nor is a messenger greater than the one who sent him'" (John 13:15–16).

The best leaders lead with the heart of a servant. That's how Jesus led and that's how He expects us to lead.

That reminds me of a Starbucks barista I met in Manila.

A few years ago, a strange thing happened on the way to my Victory Manila church staff meeting: no traffic. As a result, I arrived unusually early and had thirty minutes to kill. At the time, our church was on the fourth floor of the Robinsons Galleria mall in Manila. Rather than sitting alone and waiting for the others to arrive, I decided to walk through the empty mall to Starbucks for some much-needed morning caffeine.

When I arrived at Starbucks, though, half of the lights were off and the sign said, "Closed."

I stuck my head in the door, smiled, and spoke to the girl in the green apron who was busy behind the counter.

"Excuse me, are you open?" The store was obviously not open, but I asked anyway.

With a bright toothy smile, she energetically answered, "Sorry sir, we don't open until 9:00, but you can come in anyway. What can I get for you?"

Five minutes later, I was walking back to my staff meeting, sipping an extra hot cappuccino in a white-and-green paper cup with my name scribbled on it.

In the staff meeting, I told our team that I had just encountered a real leader—at Starbucks.

The barista could have ignored me and kept the rules. She could have told me to read the sign and wait until 9:00. But instead, she bent the rules in order to serve a customer.

Real leadership, whether in a coffee shop, a home, a boardroom, or a church, is about serving. If we have a heart to serve, we will find a way to serve and get the job done. If we don't have a heart to serve, we will find ways to avoid serving, sometimes hiding behind the letter of the law as an excuse.

Like the Starbucks barista, Jesus sometimes broke the rules in order to serve. For example, when He healed a lame man on a Sabbath (John 5), He broke the traditional Sabbath rule, explaining that the rule was made for people, not people for the rule.

More often than not, people want to lead, but they don't want to serve.

COMPLETELY MISSING THE POINT

The desire to lead without serving is not new. Some of Jesus' own disciples were more interested in climbing the leadership ladder to greatness than humbling themselves and serving. "And they came to Capernaum. And when he was in the house he asked them, 'What were you discussing on the way?' But they kept silent, for on the way *they had argued with one another about who was the greatest*" (Mark 9:33–34).

The timing of this argument about greatness among the disciples is interesting because it came shortly after Jesus had taken Peter, James, and John with Him to the Mount of Transfiguration. It was a huge moment for those three disciples. Jesus had chosen only three of the twelve to go with Him to the top of the mountain to see and experience another level of His glory. Plus, they got to meet two of their heroes, Moses and Elijah.

It's easy to see how this exclusive experience would possibly cause "the big three" to think more highly of themselves than they should have. It's clear that Peter, James, and John were beginning to form Jesus' inner circle of disciples. Maybe the dispute on the road to Capernaum came from jealousy that nine of the disciples weren't invited to meet Moses and Elijah. Or maybe, it's because the other three were boasting about their experience. More than likely, it was both.

Interestingly, Jesus didn't deal directly with the jealousy of the nine or the boasting of the three. Instead, He dealt with all of them on their misunderstanding of leadership. "And he sat down and called the twelve. And he said to them, 'If anyone would be first, he must be last of all and servant of all'" (Mark 9:35).

Jesus basically sat them down and said, "You're all missing the point! Andrew, Philip, Bartholomew, Matthew, Thomas, James, Thaddaeus, Simon, Judas—you guys want to be in the inner circle because you think that leadership and position is the *end* goal. But leadership is actually a *means* to serve God and His people. Peter, James, John—you guys are so impressed with yourselves for being part of 'the big three' that you've totally missed the point. I'm putting you in positions of leadership so that you can serve."

I'm sure they got the point now, right? No, not even close, because the same issue shows up in the next chapter.

> And James and John, the sons of Zebedee, came up to him and said to him, "Teacher, we want you to do for us whatever we ask of you." And he said to them, "What do you want me to do for you?" And they said to him, "Grant us to sit, one at your right hand and one at your left, in your glory." (Mark 10:35–37)

They thought they were asking for leadership positions, not realizing that they were completely confused about the heart of leadership. Jesus attempts to clear up their confusion. "Jesus said to them, 'You do not know what you are asking. Are you able to drink the cup that I drink, or to be baptized with the baptism with which I am baptized?'" (Mark 10:38)

They thought they knew what they were talking about, but Jesus corrected them, "You do not know what you are asking . . ."

What did they actually ask for? "Grant us to sit, one at your right hand and one at your left, in your glory" (Mark 10:37).

In their way of thinking, leadership essentially included three things:

- Position ("Grant us to sit, one at your right hand and one at your left . . .")
- Glory (". . . in your glory.")
- Authority (The seats on Jesus' right and left were seats of authority.)

"And when the ten heard it, they began to be indignant at James and John" (Mark 10:41).

THE OPPOSITE OF AUTHORITARIAN LEADERSHIP

When we reduce leadership to position, glory, and especially authority, we usually end up with a lot of indignant and angry people who argue and fight for their place in the pecking order. And this arguing and fighting for authority always results in relational pain and dysfunction. Jesus promptly corrected the disciples' wrong thinking about leadership and authority.

> And Jesus called them to him and said to them, "You know that those who are considered rulers of the Gentiles lord it over them, and their great ones exercise authority over them. But it shall not be so among you. But whoever would be great among you must be your *servant*, and whoever would be first among you must be *slave* of all. For even the Son of Man came not to be served but to serve, and to give his life as a ransom for many." (Mark 10:42–45)

Jesus said that Gentiles, or those seemingly far from God, see leadership as position, glory, and especially authority. But for those who follow Jesus, "it shall not be so among you."

After explaining that leadership is not primarily about authority, Jesus then uses two powerful word pictures to describe godly leadership to His disciples: servant and slave. No one following Jesus aspired to be a slave or a servant.

Yet Jesus said that whoever wants to be great needs to think and act like a slave and a servant.

When I was young, in order to motivate me to study hard, my parents often told me that if I didn't do well in school, I would end up working as a ditch digger. I imagine that parents in the New Testament times might have told their kids, "If you don't do well in school, you will end up as a slave or a servant."

Jesus uses those two despised positions to paint a picture of godly leadership but, as usual, His followers completely missed the point.

In a move that would later be perfected in the reality television show *Survivor*, James and John try to join forces and oust Peter from the inner circle, assuming that Jesus probably only really had space for two VIPs on His team (one on His right and the other on His left).

This of course angered the other ten disciples (including Peter), who felt that James and John were again trying to get a leg up on the rest of the disciples. Clearly, none of them had taken to heart Jesus' message that "If anyone would be first, he must be last of all and servant of all" (Mark 9:35).

Frankly, I think we often miss the point as well when we teach this story from the Bible. I can't tell you how many times I've heard pastors (including myself) explain this text by saying, "You see here, Jesus doesn't rebuke James and John for wanting to be great, but rather, He redefines greatness by saying that we must become servants."

What's wrong with that explanation? Well, nothing really. But here's what's often implied by the pastor and understood by the listener in this illustration: service is the pathway to leadership. If you serve, then you'll become great. Serve, so that one day, you'll lead.

In other words, service is the means, and leadership is the end.

As good as that sounds, it's not what Jesus was saying. In fact, it's the exact opposite of what Jesus was trying to teach His disciples.

Jesus makes it clear that He came to serve. Serving and saving sinful humanity was an end in itself—not a means to leadership and greatness. For Jesus, leading and influencing was a means to serve. Not vice versa. When correcting the way the disciples thought about leadership, service, and greatness, Jesus suggested that their desire for greatness looked a lot like the desires of the despised Gentile leaders of the day—wanting leadership for the sake of leadership. The disciples were thinking like people who grasp position and authority not to serve others, but to have others serve them.

Sadly, this faulty leadership idea that the disciples had in the first century is still present among disciples in the twenty-first century.

A HEART TO SERVE

It's not easy to find men and women who understand that leadership is first and foremost about serving. But they do exist. When I think about leaders with servant hearts, I'm reminded of my friend Paolo Punzalan.

In 1998, Paolo and his wife Jenn moved from Manila to St. Petersburg, Russia, to serve with our Every Nation church-planting team there for one year. They were not paid staff, so they rented out their house in Manila and lived off of the money they made from the tenants. They enjoyed their time in the frozen north and were considering extending their time in Russia.

Meanwhile, back in Manila, I was leading a Victory congregation that was meeting in the ballroom of the Valle Verde Country Club. At the time, our church was growing, and we desperately needed a children's pastor. Our previous children's pastor, Rommel Cervantes, was also part of the St. Petersburg team and had married a Latvian during his time there, so we didn't have much hope that he would return. In his absence, we had tried multiple children's pastors (who were all good people), but none felt called to the role long-term. It was obvious to me that it was time to find a permanent replacement for Rommel.

I called members of our small staff together and asked them to make a list of ten possible children's pastors—people who were either currently on staff or who were thinking about pursuing vocational ministry. As we went through the list, we began crossing off names one by one—some on the list were already transitioning into other areas of ministry; others simply didn't seem like the right fit.

Finally, we arrived at the tenth name on the list: Paolo Punzalan, who was twenty-seven years old. I didn't know Paolo very well at the time, but at the recommendation of our team, I called him to see if he would be interested.

Paolo was surprised by my call and quickly told me that besides raising his two-year-old son, he had absolutely zero experience with children. He had volunteered to work with the youth in the past and had some experience working with young married couples, but he had absolutely no experience in children's ministry. He had never even volunteered in the department.

But I felt like he was the man for the job. So I cut off his disclaimers and told him: "Children's ministry skills can be learned. What we are really looking for is a heart to serve."

Paolo said he could do that, so we hired him.

I think Paolo is the best children's pastor ever. Maybe I feel that way because of his influence on my sons when they were in Victory's children's church.

In the eleven-year period that Paolo served as our children's pastor, from 1998 to 2009, Victory Manila grew from 5,000 people to over 37,000 in attendance. Imagine the constantly growing number of volunteers that Paolo and his team had to recruit, equip, empower, and oversee.

Our children's ministry was never a Sunday babysitting session; it was a time to disciple and equip the next generation. In fact, our children's ministry was so dynamic that many families started coming to our church because their children asked to join. What's more, Paolo was not only able to minister to thousands of children over that period (including my children), but he was also able to train hundreds of children's ministry teachers and volunteers. That training was vital as our church grew in the early 2000s and expanded to different parts of the city.

Paolo's leadership ability was certainly developed over the years. On several occasions, we sent him to some of the best and largest children's ministries in the world, including Metro Ministries in Brooklyn, Northpoint in Atlanta, and Saddleback in California. But the foundation to his leadership development was his heart to serve.

When he took the job as the children's pastor at Victory Valle Verde, Paolo had no aspirations of moving on to higher levels of church leadership. He was there to serve and disciple kids as long as he was needed. As he spent more time in children's ministry, he began to think that he would spend the rest of his life as a children's pastor. His several visits to Metro Ministries with Bill Wilson made a deep impact on his life and ministry, and he became convinced that he was in it for the long haul. This sentiment was certainly different from the common idea that pastoral roles to oversee children and youth are just stepping stones to higher levels of leadership.

In 2008, Joey Bonifacio, then senior pastor of the Victory Fort congregation, asked Paolo if he would consider preaching at some of the newly launched Sunday evening services. He could still do children's ministry during the morning services and preach at the evening services.

Paolo agreed but was hesitant to minister to adults, as he had grown so accustomed to ministering to children. He adjusted quickly and became a fixture at the Fort's evening services. As the evening services grew and multiplied, Joey asked Paolo to take on more responsibility as the lead pastor of the evening services. However, this new responsibility would mean that he would have to stop doing children's ministry.

At first, Paolo was very reluctant. He had no desire to stop leading the children's ministry. He had committed the last decade of his life to pastoring children, and he was prepared to commit the rest of his life to it. However, as he prayed through the decision and looked at the quality of his team and possible replacements, he eventually agreed to make the transition.

After serving as lead pastor of our Victory Fort evening services, Paolo now serves as senior pastor of our entire Victory Fort congregation, which has over 16,000 people in weekend attendance.

During his time as a volunteer missionary in Russia, a children's pastor at Victory Valle Verde, and lead pastor and senior pastor at Victory Fort, Paolo's heart has only been to serve. And this has made him a great leader.

SERVANT LEADERS: MADE IN CHINA

Being a servant leader requires humility. And when I think about humble servant leaders, I'm reminded of some of my Chinese friends.

Several years ago, Victory Manila was honored to host a small invitation-only meeting that included Filipino-Chinese business leaders, pastors of the largest Chinese underground house-church movements, and Brother Yun (a.k.a. "The Heavenly Man").

As usual, the Chinese pastors arrived quite early to the meeting. When I arrived twenty minutes early to check on the sound system and set-up, I noticed that six of our honored guests, the Chinese pastors, were busy helping our Filipino ushers arrange the chairs. These pastors were responsible for establishing and leading thousands of churches representing millions of believers, and they were stacking the chairs with our ushers.

Perhaps that's odd behavior for Western megachurch pastors, but it's perfectly normal for leaders of multi-million member Chinese house-church movements. It's also normative behavior for pastors and apostles in the New Testament.

Christians from all over the world, and especially pastors, could learn a great deal about humility and servant leadership from Chinese pastors.

When I think about our pastors in China, I am reminded of Jesus' leadership perspective:

> . . . who, though he was in the form of God, did not count equality with God a thing to be grasped, but emptied

himself, by *taking the form of a servant*, being born in the likeness of men. And being found in human form, *he humbled himself* by becoming obedient to the point of death, even death on a cross. (Philippians 2:6–8)

Once we've learned to think like a leader, the next step is to act like a leader. Chapter 2 will break down exactly what it means to act like a leader.

DISCUSSION QUESTIONS X

1. Do you see serving as a means to leadership, or do you see leadership as a means to serving? What is the difference? Why does it matter?
2. Describe a leader you work with who exemplifies servant leadership.
3. Why do you want to be a leader? What motivates your desire to lead others?

2

HOW TO ACT LIKE A LEADER

Coming together is a beginning. Keeping together is progress. Working together is success.

HENRY FORD
Founder of the Ford Motor Company

The best test of whether one is qualified to lead, is to find out whether anyone is following.

D. E. HOSTE, Missionary

Moses chose able men out of all Israel and made them heads over the people, chiefs of thousands, of hundreds, of fifties, and of tens.

EXODUS 18:25

As I mentioned in the introduction, rapidly growing churches and ministries will encounter serious problems if internal leadership development does not keep pace with external growth and expansion. That's the multiplication challenge. Growing organizations rarely need more people with leadership titles, but they always need more people who act like leaders, with or without a title.

This chapter offers a simple one-sentence solution to the ever-present leadership shortage: *If you want more leaders, you need to find more people who act like leaders.* Simple enough, but how does a leader act? This chapter will attempt to answer that million-dollar question.

YOU DON'T NEED A TITLE TO ACT LIKE A LEADER

In his classic book *Spiritual Leadership,* J. Oswald Sanders tells a story that gets to the heart of how we can know if someone is acting like a leader.

About eighty years ago, a group of veteran missionaries were discussing the leadership needs in a fledgling Chinese church. When the discussion got to the topic of qualifications for leadership, the debate became intense. Everyone seemed to have a different opinion about who was qualified to lead and who was not.

One man sat silently, listening to every opinion, saying nothing. Finally, the chair asked D. E. Hoste to give his opinion. Decades ago, Hoste had responded to the gospel through the preaching of D. L. Moody. He was one of the famous "Cambridge Seven," eventually becoming the successor to Hudson Taylor as the leader of the China Inland Mission. Needless to say, the whole room listened when this missionary legend spoke: "It occurs to me that perhaps the best test of whether one is qualified to lead, is to find out whether anyone is following."

Some of the best leaders during my lifetime didn't actually have leadership authority, position, or titles, but they acted like leaders anyway, and they certainly had followers. Consider what the following people accomplished by acting like leaders, even though they didn't have leadership positions.

- **Nelson Mandela.** Most people know Mandela as the first black president to be elected in South Africa. While he accomplished much during his five years in office, his pre-presidency leadership was the foundation for all of his presidential success. Before serving as president, he served twenty-seven years as a political prisoner on Robben Island and in Pollsmoor Prison. Long before he was president, Mandela acted like a leader. With no office, no authority, and no title, he changed his nation and the world from a prison cell. He received more than 250 honors, including the 1993 Nobel Peace Prize, the US Presidential Medal of Freedom, and the Soviet Lenin Peace Prize. Why? Because he acted like a leader long before he had the title or position.

- **Ninoy Aquino.** Deborah and I arrived in Manila in 1984, nine months after the assassination of Ninoy Aquino. For the next few years, we were eyewitnesses to the power of his leadership, as even after his death, his followers toppled the corrupt Marcos regime. Aquino spent over seven years as a political prisoner and three years in exile in the United States, but the fact that he had no title, position, or authority didn't stop him from acting like a leader and changing his nation.

- **Jimmy Carter.** Most US presidents who run for re-election win. But in 1980, President Jimmy Carter left the White House in humiliation after a landslide defeat at the hands of Ronald Reagan. After that, Carter seemed to disappear from the public eye for several years. In 1984,

THE MULTIPLICATION CHALLENGE

news reports surfaced of him building houses for the poor as a volunteer carpenter with Habitat for Humanity. Ten years later, President Bill Clinton secretly commissioned Carter to negotiate a nuclear treaty with North Korea. In the next decade, Carter did diplomatic work in the Middle East, Northern Africa, South Africa, Haiti, Cuba, and Vietnam. Some historians believe that Carter accomplished more with his post-presidency diplomacy than when he actually had the job, title, position, office, and authority. Why? Because he acted like a leader.

Do you want to be a leader? Then start leading. It's that simple. It's also difficult, costly, time-consuming, and sometimes painful. But you need to stop waiting around for someone to give you a title, a salary, a budget, a staff, an office, and a website. You just need to start leading—now, not tomorrow.

WHO SHOULD I LEAD?

First, lead yourself. Motivate yourself. Encourage yourself. Strengthen yourself. Build yourself up. Self-control is foundational to leadership.

Then, if you have kids, lead your kids. Leadership starts at home. If we can't lead those closest to us (and smaller than us), then we shouldn't attempt to lead others.

Next, lead anyone who happens to see your example at work, on campus, at church, or in the gym. Leadership is by example, not by position. When people see a worthy example, they instinctively follow that example. That's leadership in action.

Notice the power of leadership by example in this passage from the book of Judges: ". . . the leaders *took the lead* in Israel . . . the people offered themselves willingly"

(Judges 5:2). In other words, as soon as the leaders started leading, the people started following. As long as no one takes the lead, no one will follow. Are you willing to take the lead? As soon as you do, people will be willing to follow.

Here's another leadership lesson from Judges: "The leaders of the people of Gilead said to each other, 'Whoever will *take the lead* attacking the Ammonites will be head over all who live in Gilead'" (Judges 10:18, NIV). In other words, whoever acts like a leader will be recognized as a leader.

There's that phrase again, "take the lead." It is as if Samuel (or whoever wrote the book of Judges) is pleading with someone—anyone—to take the lead while everyone else is standing around complaining about the situation and doing nothing.

Why are potential leaders so hesitant to take the lead? We could come up with thousands of answers to that question, but if we want to build a leadership-development culture, then we need to remove every obstacle and reject every excuse that hinders potential leaders from taking the lead.

Do you want to be a leader? Then it's time to take the lead and act like a leader.

What does it mean to act like a leader? What do leaders actually do? This chapter offers three answers to that question: leaders build, lead, and trust their team.

LEADERS BUILD THEIR TEAM

A couple of years ago during a conference in Indonesia, I was having lunch with a group of Every Nation pastors from China, Taiwan, the Philippines, and Malaysia. I was supposed to be mentoring these young ministers, but as is often the case when I meet with Asian leaders, I think I learned more from them than they learned from me.

While feasting on spicy *nasi goreng* (fried rice), *gado-gado* (steamed vegetables), *satay* (grilled meat), and peanut sauce, a young Chinese pastor shared the "five togethers" that serve as a guideline for Every Nation pastors in China. He joked that since the official Chinese government-sanctioned church is called the "The Three-Self Church," the Every Nation churches should be called the "Five-Together" churches.

The following five commitments have helped our churches in China grow strong and healthy. This list is not something our pastors have printed on websites and banners. Rather, it's a set of commitments that guides their daily lives. I think these five leadership principles can upgrade any leadership team anywhere in the world.

1. **Stay together.** First of all, the Chinese pastors committed to stay together. No matter what, they agreed not to quit or separate because of offense. Instead, they decided to forgive, repent, work it out, and keep the unity. No matter what, they decided to stay together.

2. **Grow together.** Secondly, they committed to grow together. For them, as leaders, spiritual status quo was not an option. They acknowledged their need to grow in knowledge, character, and competency. And they all agreed that the best spiritual growth happens when we do life and theology together, not when we attempt to do life alone.

3. **Dream together.** Thirdly, they committed to dream together. Every time I get around other leaders, my faith is stretched and my vision expands. Left to myself, I'm content with small vision and small dreams. Maybe that's

because I know that dreams and vision create more work, and sometimes I want to avoid more work. All leaders need a group of peers to stretch their faith, to rebuke their unbelief, and to challenge them to dream bigger.

4. Work together. Next, these young Chinese pastors committed to work together. They knew that the task of reaching their nation of one billion people was way too big to do alone. The magnitude of the job demanded that they work together. Scripture teaches that "Two are better than one, because they have a good reward for their toil" (Ecclesiastes 4:9). In other words, two get more done than one. This is not rocket science. You want to accomplish more? Build a team so you can work together, not alone.

5. Lead together. And finally, knowing that the best leadership is done in concert as a team, not as a soloist, my Chinese friends committed to lead together. Insecure and ignorant leaders lead alone. Secure and wise leaders build a leadership team. How did these Chinese pastors lead together? They wisely reasoned that the most effective way to lead together would be to stay together, grow together, dream together, and work together. The more we do life, ministry, and mission together, the better we will become as leaders.

The key word in all five commitments is obviously the word "together."

GREAT LEADERSHIP TEAMS IN THE BIBLE
The original disciples were called to walk and work together as a team. They were not called to be Lone Rangers or independent contractors for God. Notice that Jesus not only called His disciples to walk with Him, but He also called them

to walk together with each other. If Peter wanted to follow Jesus, he had to follow along with James, Nathaniel, and Judas. Jesus never offered anyone the option of following Him alone. "And he called the twelve *together* and gave them power and authority over all demons and to cure diseases, and he sent them out to proclaim the kingdom of God and to heal" (Luke 9:1–2).

People called to ministry typically like the idea of "power and authority over all demons," but they sometimes fail to notice that the "power and authority" follows the "together" part of Luke 9. If you are called to power and authority, then you are called together with others of like calling. No one is called to wander around trying to accomplish God's will alone. Here are some great examples of leading together in the Bible:

- **Moses.** Moses was a great leader (maybe the greatest leader in the Old Testament), but he knew better than to attempt to lead alone. He built a team that included his brother and spokesman, Aaron. Team Moses also included a dude named Hur, and a fearless young warrior named Joshua. Moses was a great leader, in part, because he had a great team. As the team leader, Moses took the blame when things went wrong and shared the honor when things went right. After a historic victory over the Amalekites, Moses summarized the battle with these words, "And Joshua overwhelmed Amalek and his people with the sword." (See Exodus 17:8–13.) Moses was secure enough to give credit for the victory to a young, next-generation leader. Are you secure enough to give credit to young leaders? Secure leaders give credit. Insecure leaders hoard credit.

- **David.** David was Israel's greatest king ever, but, like Moses, he never led alone. He had his "mighty men," who could shoot an arrow and sling a stone with the right and left hand. David's team was led by an executive committee of three that was chaired by Jashobeam the Hachmonite. Read that name again, real slow. *Jashobeam the Hachmonite, a.k.a. "The Beam."* That's a leader's name if I ever heard one. In one famous battle, The Beam killed 300 enemy warriors with his spear, all by himself. If I'm ever in a war, I think I want someone like Jashobeam the Hachmonite on my team. David was a great leader because he surrounded himself with great men.

- **Daniel.** Daniel's team included his best friends, Hananiah, Mishael, and Azariah (a.k.a. Shadrach, Meshach, and Abednego). Daniel knew he would need a team in order to successfully overcome the temptations of Babylon. Ultimately, he and his friends not only endured temptation together, but were recognized by their leaders and peers as ten times better than all the other young men in Babylon. They had hoped that they would be "better together" and they were. (See Daniel 1:11–20.)

- **Jesus.** Even Jesus refused to do ministry alone. He had His twelve, plus a larger team of seventy. If anyone could have done it alone, it would have been Jesus, but He spent three years building a team.

Leadership is supposed to be plural. If you are called to lead, then you are called to build a team so you can lead together. That's a good thing, because all of us will always be better together.

GREAT LEADERS: DISCOVERED OR DEVELOPED?

Victory Manila's rapid growth revealed an urgent leadership shortage that forced us to revisit our leadership-development strategy. Nevertheless, even in our leadership-crisis phase, we still had more leaders than some. I realized this fact when pastors from around the world would visit our church and inevitably comment on the number and quality of our leaders. We thought we had a leadership shortage, but our visitors saw leaders everywhere.

Visiting leaders would often ask where we found so many leaders, as if leaders are simply waiting around to be discovered. Others, realizing that leaders are developed and not discovered, asked about our leadership-development materials. A few bold pastors asked if they could hire some of our leaders. Their reasoning: Victory had so many leaders; surely we could offer a few to the highest bidder?

Since Victory Manila started in 1984, we have rarely *found* or *discovered* leaders. That might be because we have never attempted to solve our leadership shortage by looking for or recruiting leaders.

While we have not *discovered* very many leaders, we have *developed* thousands. Most of the leaders we developed did not even remotely resemble leaders when we started working with them. But isn't that how most great leaders in the Bible started?

No one but Jesus would have picked the twelve people He did to be the original leaders of the church. To the untrained eye, they had zero leadeship potential.

Think about David's mighty men. Many of them were hiding in a cave, depressed, in debt, and bitter when he found them. (See 1 Samuel 22.) David did not discover leaders in a cave. He developed leaders by doing life together (or more accurately, by running for their lives together).

Everywhere the Apostle Paul ministered, leadership happened. Notice how Paul described the starting point of the Corinthian leaders:

> For consider your calling, brothers: not many of you were wise according to worldly standards, not many were powerful, not many were of noble birth. But God chose what is foolish in the world to shame the wise; God chose what is weak in the world to shame the strong; God chose what is low and despised in the world, even things that are not, to bring to nothing things that are . . . (1 Corinthians 1:26–28)

Paul didn't find very many ready-made leaders. He found plenty of people who were not wise, not strong, and not noble. But after being transformed by the gospel, investing in the mission, and participating in a local church community, many of them eventually became great leaders.

If you want to act like a leader, then don't lead alone. Build a team. Don't recruit or hire a team of current leaders. Instead, identify potential leaders, and take the necessary time to develop them into a great team.

LEADERS LEAD THEIR TEAM

Teams need leaders. Strong teams need strong leaders. Great teams need great leaders. Productive teams need productive leaders. Spiritual teams need spiritual leaders. Apostolic teams need apostolic leaders.

If you want to act like a leader, first build your team, then lead your team. Everyone on the team can and should have a voice, but all voices are not equal in wisdom and authority. At the end of the day, teams still need to be led.

Jesus, the greatest leader ever, built His team, and then He led it. If you want to be a leader, and if you want to multiply leaders, then follow Jesus' example. Build your team, then graciously and unapologetically lead it.

How can a leader build and lead a strong healthy team of leaders? Here are three tools to help leaders lead their teams.

1. **Energy.** One of the most important things a leader brings to the team is energy. Paul exhorted the Roman believers, "Do not be slothful in zeal, be fervent in spirit, serve the Lord" (Romans 12:11). Slothfulness and leadership are like oil and water. They don't mix. Slothfulness is the complete opposite of leadership. I've sometimes witnessed leaders who attempted to mix the two. They're slothful in the way they lead meetings, prepare sermons, and communicate their vision. They have low energy. The NIV translation of Romans 12:11 says, "Never be lacking in zeal." Leaders should be zealous all the time. They must bring energy to every meeting and every situation. Energy can be loud or quiet, demonstrative or cool, but it's always fully engaged. Energy has nothing to do with personality. If you want to lead your team, you better show up with energy (a.k.a. zeal), even if you are jetlagged and exhausted.

2. **Clarity.** To effectively lead a strong team, the leader must function as the CCO, or the Chief Clarity Officer (in the words of organizational health expert Patrick Lencioni). Nothing is more important to team health than the constant and repetitive creation and communication of clarity. Great leaders create clarity concerning mission, vision, values, culture, and lanes of authority. If your team is confused about mission, vision, values, culture, or lanes, it's because the CCO (the leader) has failed to create and communicate

clarity. Have you ever noticed that the yellow and white stripes denoting highway lanes tend to fade over time? Every few years, they're repainted. Then they fade and need to be repainted again, and again, and again. Likewise, time causes mission, vision, values, culture, and lanes to fade. Leaders need to constantly repaint the lines and recreate the lanes of clarity.

3. Unity. As the father of three young, energetic boys, creating and enforcing unity was a daily chore for many years. As soon as one conflict was resolved and unity was restored, another situation would arise. As a ministry leader with hundreds of strong leaders all over the world, I'm still creating and enforcing unity. If the team is not in unity, it's the leader's fault. Leaders create unity by example, explanation, experience, and sometimes, expulsion. They must set an example of maintaining unity even when they disagree. Leaders can maintain unity by explaining the greater cause and the bigger picture, and they bring to the team years of wisdom that can only be gained by experience. Sometimes, the only way a leader can create unity is by expelling an irreconcilable person from the team. Paul said it like this, "Make every effort to keep the unity of the Spirit through the bond of peace" (Ephesians 4:3, NIV). Creating and keeping unity requires effort, and that's what leaders do.

LEADERS TRUST THEIR TEAM

Several years ago, during the week of Victory Manila's twenty-five year anniversary festivities, my coauthor and oldest son, William, conducted a series of extensive interviews with our Victory pastors. The goal was to identify some of the foundational principles that contributed to our Victory leadership culture.

Every leader he interviewed told at least one story about how trust made an impact on them and shaped their lives and their approach to leadership. Several said that even when they were immature and seemingly untrustworthy, they were entrusted with important ministry responsibilities anyway.

As I read William's summary of the interviews, I was shocked by how something as simple as trust could make such a great impact on young men with leadership potential. Today, they're no longer young men, and they're no longer future leaders or potential leaders. They're some of the greatest leaders I know anywhere in the world. And they insist that being trusted helped them become leaders.

It's humbling to realize that my trust helped them become the leaders they are today. It's also humbling to admit that my trust, more than my preaching and teaching, helped them become great leaders. All this time, I thought I was pretty good at leadership training. In reality, I was good at leadership trusting.

In order to explain what it means for a leader to trust a team, let me share some stories from a long time ago, and some excerpts from William's interviews.

In 1984, the church that would one day be known as Victory Manila was one month old. Our "leadership team" consisted of students who had been around for about three weeks, plus a few American missionaries who volunteered to stay an extra month to help our little church.

After four weeks in the Philippines, Rice Broocks, my good friend who had organized the trip, and our American team were leaving. Deborah and I were about to be left behind.

As soon as the Korean Airlines plane carrying Rice and the American summer missionaries left Philippine airspace, I gathered our fledgling leadership team and said, "Rice and the team are gone. Someone has to preach. Who has a word from God?"

Immediately, one of the American missionaries who had stayed behind an extra month eagerly volunteered. I have only a vague recollection of the incident, but according to Jun Escosar, I ignored the mature missionary, turned to Jun and asked him to prepare a message. Jun said he was both shocked and encouraged that I was so quick to trust him with this level of responsibility. During his interview for the twenty-fifth anniversary, Jun told William, "Your dad was a risk-taker, and he took a risk with us. I'm so glad he did." I didn't see it as risky because I trusted Jun. More importantly, I trusted the Holy Spirit in him. Three decades later, Dr. Jun Escosar is a respected missiologist and serves as Every Nation's regional director for Asia. It's an honor to work with Jun and to call him a friend.

Here's another story of what it looks like to trust your team.

Ferdie Cabiling was one of our 1984 originals at Victory. He was also, along with Jun, one of our original staff members. For many years, I was the pastor and Ferdie was my designated evangelist. No matter what my sermon topic, I would end by giving the mic to Ferdie, who would then preach a two-minute gospel message and call people to Christ. I loved tag-team preaching with Ferdie. (Every pastor should have an evangelist on staff to end each sermon.)

Eventually, I asked Ferdie if he would serve as senior pastor of our newly planted congregation at the Music Museum auditorium in Greenhills. At the time, I was leading our afternoon congregation in Valle Verde and our evening congregation at Music Museum. Ferdie declined my offer, insisting that he only wanted to work as part of my team.

When it came time for our annual summer trip to the States to visit mission partners and family, I asked Ferdie to take charge of Music Museum until I returned. This time, he didn't really have a choice, so Ferdie reluctantly agreed to hold down the fort for two months.

After eight weeks, I returned with a gift for Ferdie: a No Fear T-shirt that said, "Lead, follow, or get the @&%#$ out of the way." He got the message that I believed in him as a leader, and he decided to lead. Today, he oversees all twenty-five Victory Manila locations, including several hundred staff members and 137 worship services.

Here's one final trust-your-team story.

Like Ferdie, when I first met Robert Hern, Jr., he was a teenager. Over the years, Robert has served as a worship leader, church planter, world conference coordinator, Every Nation Philippines operations director, and finally, as the senior pastor of our Pioneer congregation. When we asked Robert to lead Victory Pioneer, he was hesitant and said "No thanks" several times. Finally, after our persistence, he agreed.

During his interview, Robert told William, "They saw something in me that I didn't see. And I trusted what they saw in me."

What we saw in him is called leadership potential. You will have to wait until chapter 6 to see the results of Robert's leadership potential. I'll give you a hint. He recently started a new church in San Diego, California.

I love Robert's next-generation leadership philosophy: "There's a big difference between having young people in your church and having young people leading your church."

I can't wait to see what God does in San Diego with a church not only filled with young people, but with a church-leadership team that makes room for young people. Jesus trusted young leaders. We should follow Robert's example and trust them, too. We will talk more about trusting young leaders later.

LEADERSHIP IS RELATIONSHIP

My good friend Joey Bonifacio, a Victory pastor and author of the discipleship book *The Lego Principle*, always says, "Discipleship is relationship." I agree with Joey. And I also believe that leadership is relationship.

Jesus seemed to take a relational rather than a positional approach to leadership. Before Jesus was crucified, Peter denied Him. It's difficult for modern Western Christians to understand the significance of the sin of denial. We understand the gravity of murder and adultery, but not denial. In Peter's world, denial was no minor infraction; rather, it was at the top of the pyramid of horrible sins.

John 21 records Jesus interacting with Peter after his denial. Notice that Jesus first restores the relationship, then the ministry. Why? Because discipleship is relationship, and leadership is relationship. If Peter wanted to continue to be a disciple, and if he wanted to make disciples, and if he wanted to have a leadership role in the church, his relationship with Jesus had to be restored.

Jesus asked a variation of the same question three times. "Do you love me?" This is a relational question, not a ministerial question. Jesus did not ask about ministry, vision, strategy, or mission.

After Peter answered the relational question, then (and only then) did Jesus mention a new ministry assignment: "Feed my lambs, take care of my sheep, feed my sheep . . ."

Once we get the relationships right, discipleship and leadership will naturally follow. Strong and healthy relationships produce strong and healthy leaders because leadership is relationship.

As soon as we start acting like a leader, it's essential that we learn to listen like a leader. The next chapter will explain the power of listening and will give a list of the most important voices a leader must listen to and consider.

DISCUSSION QUESTIONS X

1. What are the benefits and dangers of someone leading without a title or position?
2. Do you tend to trust or micromanage those you lead? What are the potential pitfalls of both?
3. What are ways you can bring energy to your team?
4. Do you look for already-developed leaders around you, or do you look for individuals with potential to develop into great leaders? Why?

3

HOW TO LISTEN LIKE A LEADER

Courage is what it takes to stand up and speak;
courage is also what it takes to sit down and listen.
WINSTON CHURCHILL
Former Prime Minister of the United Kingdom

This is why he [Coach Steve Kerr] is the greatest
boss in the world. We can all make suggestions,
even a video guy, and he'll seriously consider them.
LUKE WALTON, Basketball Coach

Everyone should be quick to listen, slow to speak
and slow to become angry.
JAMES 1:19 (NIV)

It's not every day that you see an article about a basketball team in the *Wall Street Journal.* But on June 12, 2015, the *Wall Street Journal* ran an article with the title, "How a Twenty-Eight-Year-Old Assistant May Have Saved Golden State."

For those who don't follow American basketball, the Golden State Warriors won the 2015 NBA Finals and a lot of the credit goes to a young man who was neither a coach nor a player.

WHEN LEADERS LISTEN, THE WHOLE TEAM WINS

The twenty-eight-year-old who saved the Warriors is Nick U'Ren, special assistant to Steve Kerr, the head coach. As the head coach's assistant, during games, Nick sits behind the bench working on his laptop. Before games, he rebounds as Warriors' superstar Steph Curry practices his three-point shot. Between games, he edits team videos. In the off-season, he manages Steve Kerr's travel schedule.

So, how did Nick U'Ren save Golden State's championship season? Here's the story. During the 2014–2015 season, Golden State had the best record in the NBA. They breezed through the early rounds of the playoffs with ease. But the first three games of the Finals were a different story. For the first time all year, they looked like mortals as LeBron James and his Cleveland Cavs manhandled the once-unstoppable Warriors.

The NBA Finals uses a best-of-seven format, meaning the first team to win four games is the champion. Going into Game 4, the Cavs were up two games to one. Most commentators saw Game 4 as a must-win for the Warriors. Coach Steve Kerr knew that something needed to change, but he wasn't sure exactly what.

The night before the fourth game, while watching a video of the 2014 NBA Finals between the San Antonio Spurs and the Miami Heat, U'Ren got a crazy idea to contain LeBron and beat the Cavs. In 2014, the Spurs were able to beat LeBron and his former team, the Miami Heat, by playing "small ball," which basically means benching their big men and replacing them with smaller, quicker players. U'Ren called assistant coach Luke Walton and made a suggestion: bench seven-foot tall Andrew Bogut, who had been the 2005 overall first draft pick and had started sixty-five games, and replace him with six-foot-six Andre Aguodala, who had started zero games for the Warriors.

It didn't take long for U'Ren to convince Walton, who then texted Coach Kerr at three o'clock in the morning with the radical idea. At breakfast the next morning, twelve hours before the crucial Game 4, the coaches discussed all possible plans to stop or even contain LeBron and the Cavs. After hearing every suggestion, Kerr decided to go with the special assistant's plan.

It worked. Aguodala guarded LeBron and held him to just twenty points, plus Aguodala scored twenty-two points, and Golden State won Game 4. They also won Games 5 and 6 and the 2015 NBA Finals championship with their "small ball" line-up. But that's not all. Aguodala, a guy who hadn't started one game the entire season until Game 4 of the Finals, won the MVP trophy.

After the victory, Golden State Warriors' owner Joe Lacob congratulated Coach Kerr with two words: "Good coaching."

Yes, it was good coaching. But the good coaching happened long before Kerr decided to replace a seven-foot player with a six-foot-six player, long before the Game 4 victory, and long before the first game of the season. Good coaching and good leadership always start by building a good team.

As soon as Kerr became the Warriors' head coach, he immediately started building his team, which included two veteran coaches, Ron Adams and Alvin Gentry. To this core, he added two young coaches, Luke Walton and

Jarron Collins. And of course, he added special assistant Nick U'Ren, who had worked for him in Phoenix. Then, he created an atmosphere where the whole team felt free to talk, and he would listen.

I don't know if he realized it or not, but by listening to Nick U'Ren, Coach Kerr was borrowing a play out of President Abraham Lincoln's playbook. During his presidency, from 1861 until he was assassinated in 1865, Lincoln frequently opened the White House to anyone who wanted to present an idea or express an opinion. While Lincoln certainly did not agree with every opinion offered, he listened, always trying to learn something new. Lincoln credited what he called his "public-opinion baths" with helping him to stay in touch with the people he was elected to lead. He also constantly asked for the opinions and ideas of random people whom he met along the way, resulting in a flood of letters from average citizens to the White House. Lincoln was a great leader, in part, because he was a great listener.

If learning to listen can help a coach win the NBA Finals and a president lead a nation, imagine how it could help you lead your church, campus ministry, or organization.

LEADERS LISTEN

A few years ago, a good friend gave me a not-so-subtle message for Christmas in the form of a book. I love getting books for Christmas. As soon as I tore through the red-and-green wrapping paper and saw the title, a message shouted at me loud and clear: *Listening Leaders: The 10 Golden Rules to Listen, Lead, and Succeed.*

I got it. I needed to upgrade my listening skills. I read a lot of leadership books, but I had never read one that was exclusively about listening.

As I type these words, I have a tall stack of leadership books on my desk. Some were written by famous leadership gurus, including Robert Clinton, Oswald Sanders, John Townsend, and Chris Lowney. Other titles are by less known, but equally great authors. Titles include classics like *Spiritual Leadership, LeaderShift, The Making of a Leader,* and *Heroic Leadership.* I have read some of these books over and over. Most are underlined and highlighted. Some are held together by duct tape.

As I peruse the leadership books on my desk and those still on my shelves, I'm having a difficult time finding anything about listening. It's hard to believe that so few of these leadership books (with the exception of my Christmas gift mentioned above) talk about the importance of leaders learning to listen.

However, the Bible is clear on the topic. Consider the importance of listening and the danger of not listening in the following passage.

> *But they would not listen,* but were stubborn, as their fathers had been, who did not believe in the Lord their God. . . . However, *they would not listen,* but they did according to their former manner. So these nations feared the Lord and also served their carved images. Their children did likewise, and their children's children—as their fathers did, so they do to this day. (2 Kings 17:14,40–41)

These verses reveal that an unwillingness to listen not only adversely affected those who closed their ears, but also made a negative impact on future generations for many years.

I often meet with potential leaders, future leaders, and next-generation leaders. Sometimes, these meetings are scheduled. Other times, they're spontaneous. Recently, during a mentorship moment at a coffee shop with a young leader, I noticed that he looked at his phone while I was talking. I ignored his impulsive reflex and continued our conversation, asking questions, and listening to his answers. Ten minutes later, he looked at his phone again while I was talking to him. This time, he responded to the message on his screen. The third time he interacted with his phone while talking to me, I knew I had to say something. We had a blunt talk about focus, listening, and basic etiquette. My message to him was clear: If you want to learn to lead, you need to learn to listen.

He had a huge leadership gift, but it was being stunted by his inability to focus on what was in front of him and his unwillingness to listen to the person in front of him. I wasn't personally offended by his texting and tweeting while I was talking. I have thicker skin than that. I was upset because his undeveloped listening skills were holding him back from God's best for his life and calling.

His inability to ignore his phone led to a good leadership discussion about listening that included some of the following ideas:

"The way of a fool is right in his own eyes, but a wise man listens to advice" (Proverbs 12:15).

"The ear that listens to life-giving reproof will dwell among the wise" (Proverbs 15:31).

"If one gives an answer before he hears, it is his folly and shame" (Proverbs 18:13).

"Listen to advice and accept instruction, that you may gain wisdom in the future" (Proverbs 19:20).

"Cease to hear instruction, my son, and you will stray from the words of knowledge" (Proverbs 19:27).

". . . let every person be quick to hear, slow to speak, slow to anger" (James 1:19).

All these verses essentially say the same thing: listening is important. Unfortunately, listening is also rare, especially among leaders.

THE SEVEN VOICES
WISE LEADERS MUST LISTEN TO

Scripture is clear that leaders must be listeners, but with so many voices shouting so many different messages, it's important to establish which voices matter the most. I've found it helpful to intentionally listen to the following seven voices, especially when they don't totally agree with me.

1. Leaders. My friend and colleague Michael Paderes mentors young church planters and pastors all over the world. A couple of years ago, he told me about correcting a young, talented church planter who frequently displayed an arrogant know-it-all attitude. While this young pastor didn't actually know it all, he did know much more than most of his ministry peers. This smart, well-read young man also thought he knew more than many of his leaders.

Michael is a skilled mentor who never shrinks back from speaking the truth in love, even when the truth is uncomfortable. To his credit, the young leader humbly accepted Michael's correction and responded by writing a heartfelt apology and plea for continued mentoring, correction, and accountability. We all need mentors and leaders who love us enough to speak the truth in love, and we need to make sure we listen when they speak.

When we are young and new to ministry, it's easy to find leaders and mentors, and it's easy to listen to them. The longer we're in ministry and the higher we climb the leadership ladder, the more intentional we must be about seeking leaders and mentors to speak into our lives. The longer I lead, the more aware I am of my continued need for leaders and mentors, and the more difficult they are to find. Bottom line: leaders need to listen to leaders.

2. **Friends.** I have often asked my lifelong friends to correct, adjust, and balance me any time they feel I'm even slightly off. If not for honest friends, there's no telling how many bad decisions I would have made. Also, without faithful friends, I would have gone through much of my life with a bad attitude.

I'll never forget the night my good friend John Rohrer confronted my rotten attitude about something. John was in Manila to minister at Victory, and he was staying in my home. I took the opportunity to dump my complaints on him concerning one of our Victory pastors. I don't remember what the issue was, but I sure was frustrated. John listened patiently. When I finished venting, he responded, "Steve, you've crossed the line from frustration to bitterness, and the only way to solve this is for you to repent, forgive, and forget it. Your attitude is the real problem here."

That's not what I wanted to hear from John. I wanted him to agree with my bad attitude and take up my offense. Instead, he acted like a real friend and practiced Proverbs 27:5–6 on me: "Better is open rebuke than hidden love. Faithful are the wounds of a friend . . ."

I thank God that I have friends who love me enough to openly rebuke me and faithfully wound me when I need it most. All leaders need a group of friends who know and love them enough to speak the truth without worrying about offense.

My favorite Trappist monk, Thomas Merton, summarized the importance of friends who speak truth when he wrote, "May God preserve me from the love of friends who will never dare to rebuke me."

If you're a leader and you don't have friends who will dare to rebuke you, then for your own good, you need to find some today.

3. Peers. The story of King David and his drama with Bathsheba, Uriah, and Nathan—especially the part when Nathan confronts David—is a sobering picture of the importance of leaders listening to their peers. Despite his massive failures, David's mistakes were dealt with and he ended strong because of a faithful friend like Nathan and a forgiving, gracious God.

Here's my quick summary of this dark episode in David's life.

It was a season when all good kings should go off to war, but David got lazy, delegated his duty to General Joab, and took the month off. (See 2 Samuel 11:1.) While hanging out on his roof deck, David spotted a beautiful woman, Bathsheba, taking a bath and acted on a lustful impulse. We all know the rest of the story.

David got into trouble because he wasn't where he should have been. When leaders stop doing what they're supposed to do, they invite trouble. Not everything can be delegated—leaders must personally fight certain battles.

If we refuse to lead and fight, we will eventually make a mess of our lives and the lives of those around us.

No matter how determined David was to cover his sin, God loved him enough to provide a prophet named Nathan. Kings and prophets in those days had an interesting, and sometimes complicated, relationship with one another. The king was ultimately in charge, but as God's mouth-piece, the prophet often operated more like a peer than a subordinate. Every leader needs a peer like Nathan who will boldly and creatively speak uncomfortable truth. The larger the ministry and more lofty the leadership title, the less people are willing to speak truth to that leader. That's one reason so many leaders fall from such great heights. May God give all leaders modern Nathans who will tell us the painful truth in every situation.

To his credit, David confessed and repented as soon as Nathan rebuked him. Nathan's reply to David's repentance is both comforting and terrifying: "The Lord also has put away your sin; you shall not die" (2 Samuel 12:13).

I'm sure David was comforted knowing that God wasn't going to kill him. However, while forgiven, David's sin wasn't forgotten. Nathan spelled out the consequences of David's sin: Bathsheba's child would die and innocent family members would suffer horribly. (See 2 Samuel 12:11–14.)

Do you have peers in your life who have permission to speak truth, especially truth you don't want to hear? Do you listen to your peers when they attempt to speak uncomfortable truth?

4. Followers. So far, we've talked about the importance of listening to leaders, friends, and peers, but listening to these voices should be relatively easy to do. Now we get to three difficult voices that many leaders ignore to their own harm: followers, critics, and spouses. Some leaders actually believe that they should deliberately not listen to followers, critics, or spouses.

This chapter started with a story about a basketball team winning a championship because the head coach listened to a follower, someone who was several positions under him in the Golden State Warriors' organizational chart.

If any professional basketball coach had the right to not listen to the special assistant/video guy, it was coach Steve Kerr. Prior to landing the job as head coach of the Warriors, Kerr's basketball résumé was already impressive. As a college player, he led the University of Arizona to the Final Four of the National Collegiate Athletic Association (NCAA) in 1988. During his thirteen-year professional career, he won five NBA championship rings—three with the Chicago Bulls (with a little help from Michael Jordan) and two with the San Antonio Spurs. He also won the NBA three-point shootout and the NBA Shooting Stars competition. After his playing days ended, Kerr worked as a highly respected basketball analyst for Turner Network Television (TNT). After his stellar broadcasting career, he became president and general manager of the Phoenix Suns basketball organization.

Why would a guy with this much basketball experience and expertise listen to a twenty-eight-year-old special assistant and video editor? Here's how Coach Kerr answered that question: "Whoever has the right idea or a good idea—it doesn't matter where it comes from. I'm happy Nick brought it to me."

Assistant coach and former Los Angeles Lakers player Luke Walton described Kerr's leadership and decision-making culture like this: "It was his decision. It's always his decision. But this is why he's the greatest boss in the world. We can all make suggestions, even a video guy, and he'll seriously consider them."

In 1 Kings 12, we read a story about the folly of leaders ignoring the voices of the people they hope to lead. King Rehoboam had replaced his father, King Solomon, on the throne of Israel. Jeroboam and a large group of Israel's leaders approached the new king with a reasonable request. "Your father made our yoke heavy. Now therefore lighten the hard service of your father and his heavy yoke on us, and we will serve you."

To his credit, the young king allowed his followers to speak. That's more than some leaders do. After hearing their request, King Rehoboam said, "Go away for three days, then come again to me."

So far, so good. He let his followers give a suggestion and rather than immediately making a decision, he wanted to think about his answer for a few days.

During those three days, the king first sought the counsel of the old men who had advised his father, King Solomon (who was a pretty wise leader). Their advice? "If you will be a servant to this people today and serve them, and speak good words to them when you answer them, then they will be your servants forever."

The advice was good, but the young, insecure king unfortunately rejected it. "But he abandoned the counsel that the old men gave him and took counsel with the young men who had grown up with him and stood before him."

Sometimes abandoning the voice of our followers is a bad idea, especially when those followers have more experience than we do.

Do you create the kind of culture where your followers can put their ideas on the table? Do you seriously listen to them? Victories are waiting for the humble leader who will dare to listen to faithful and wise followers.

5. Critics. These voices are perhaps the most difficult to hear, especially when our critics are exaggerating, lying, or making personal attacks. I don't hate my critics, but I usually hate listening to them. When critics speak, blog, or tweet, I remind myself to ask God to help me hear the truth, even if it is not spoken in love.

Luke recorded a story of church growth in Acts that illustrates how wise church leaders should respond to critics: "Now in these days when the disciples were increasing in number, a complaint by the Hellenists arose against the Hebrews because their widows were being neglected in the daily distribution" (Acts 6:1).

Most pastors and campus missionaries wrongly assume that growth will solve all of their problems and resolve all complaints. In reality, it creates a multiplication challenge. Growth will simultaneously create new problems and expose existing problems. In other words, more growth will cause more problems and more complaints.

How should leaders respond to complaints and criticism? Notice what the apostles did when their critics spoke. First, they listened. Second, they recognized when their critics had a valid point. Third, they:

> . . . summoned the full number of the disciples and said, "It is not right that we should give up preaching the word of God to serve tables. Therefore, brothers, pick out from among you seven men of good repute, full of the Spirit and of wisdom, whom we will appoint to this duty. But we will devote ourselves to prayer and to the ministry of the word." (Acts 6:2–4)

When critics speak, secure leaders listen and respond with wisdom.

6. Your spouse. Earlier, when I mentioned the importance of listening to your friends, I recounted a time when my friend John Rohrer rebuked me for having a bad attitude about a pastor. The worst part of being rebuked by John was that he did it in front of my wife, who had more than once graciously told me exactly what John said. But, rather than listening to her and getting right with my friend and with God, I stubbornly ignored her and rationalized my sinful attitude.

Some leaders never listen to their spouses. Some spouses never speak up. The more I listen to Deborah though, the more I make better decisions. That's another way of saying that she's usually right.

You may have heard the joke about the man and his wife who created a way to make decisions without the need to talk or listen. On their wedding day, they agreed that the husband would handle all the big decisions. The wife would make all the small decisions. After twenty years of marriage, the husband was amazed that he had not had to make even one big decision.

A better way for making decisions might be for husbands and wives to actually talk, listen, and make decisions together. Ignore your spouse at your own peril.

7. God. The voice of God is the last on this list, but it's certainly not the last voice we need to listen to. In fact, there's a sense in which the voice of God is the only voice leaders need to hear and heed. The whole point of listening to the voice of our leaders, friends, peers, followers, critics, and spouses is so that we can better hear and discern God's wisdom, will, and voice.

But sometimes, God's voice is not as loud or as dramatic as we think it should be, as we see in a story about the prophet Elijah in 1 Kings 19:1–18.

Elijah was having a bad day. He had received a credible death threat from his nemesis, Jezebel. He needed to hear from God, and he was listening. Then "a great and strong wind tore the mountains and broke in pieces the rocks before the Lord, but the Lord was not in the wind." After the rock-breaking wind, Elijah experienced an earthquake and a fire, but again, the Lord was not speaking through these dramatic events. Finally, the voice of God came to Elijah in "the sound of a low whisper."

Many times I wish God would speak louder. But since He rarely yells, I realize that I need to create a quiet environment if I really want to hear him.

MULTI-GENERATIONAL LISTENING

The older I get, the more everyone seems to be talking and writing about leadership-succession planning. I'm glad for all the information that has increasingly become available. Some of it's helpful; some of it's confusing. But the truth is, I've been thinking about my Manila succession plan for over thirty years. That doesn't prove that I'm good or even marginally adequate at advanced strategic planning. I'm not. Anyone who has worked with me for more than one week can testify that I'm actually terrible at it.

I started working on my succession plan over three decades ago because I wrongly assumed that Deborah and I would only stay in Manila a few months. Operating under that belief, I figured I needed to find some next-generation leaders and start equipping and empowering them immediately. In those days, the next generation was two to five years younger than me. Now, they're twenty to thirty years younger.

I mentioned Solomon earlier in this chapter. The transition from his father, King David, to him was much better than the transition to his own son, Rehoboam, in part because Solomon understood multi-generational leadership and embraced the importance of continuity. Tragically, Rehoboam didn't get it. Consider Solomon's prayer in 2 Chronicles 1:9: "O Lord God, *let your word to David my father* be now fulfilled, for you have made me king over a people as numerous as the dust of the earth."

Unlike many leaders today, Solomon didn't pray for his own mission, vision, or word to replace the mission, vision, and word that he had heard from his father. Rather, he saw himself as a continuation of God's purpose from generation to generation. Solomon didn't need a unique or new mission, vision, or word. He discovered and understood his purpose as he listened to his father.

Solomon's multi-generational mission didn't even start with his father's generation. In the prayer cited above, Solomon recognized that it had started long before King David was on the throne. Being king over "a people as numerous as the dust of the earth" harkens back to God's promise to Abraham, Isaac, and Jacob, many generations before David was born.

Unlike his father Solomon, Rehoboam "abandoned the counsel that the old men gave him" (2 Chronicles 10:8). It's always a bad idea for a young leader to turn a deaf ear to the older people who represent previous generations.

When the leader listens, the whole team wins. As soon as we learn to listen like a leader, we will immediately start growing like a leader, which will help us rise to the multiplication challenge. The next chapter will dig deep into what it means to grow like a leader.

DISCUSSION QUESTIONS X

1. How do you respond when your leaders correct you? How do you respond when your peers/friends correct you? How do you respond to your critics?
2. Have you given anyone permission to speak into your life? Who? If not, make a list of people you will ask to do so.
3. What are the potential benefits and pitfalls of listening to your followers?
4. Do you create the kind of culture where your followers can put their ideas on the table? Do you seriously listen to them?

4

HOW TO GROW LIKE A LEADER

Leaders aren't born; they are made. And they are made just like anything else, through hard work.
VINCE LOMBARDI, Football Coach

Jesus grew in wisdom and stature, and in favor with God and man.
LUKE 2:52 (NIV)

Not only that, but we rejoice in our sufferings, knowing that suffering produces endurance, and endurance produces character, and character produces hope . . .
ROMANS 5:3–4

L eadership guru Jack Welch served as CEO of General Electric for twenty years. During his tenure, GE's value grew 4,000 percent. Since his retirement in 2001, Welch has stayed busy writing and speaking about leadership. Here's a classic Welch leadership quote: "Before you are a leader, success is all about *growing yourself.* When you become a leader, success is all about *growing others.*"

I used to love this quote, but the more I lead and develop leaders, the less I love it. I agree with Welch that before we ever become leaders, we need to focus on growing ourselves. And yes, after we attain leadership positions, we need to help others grow. But once we become leaders, it's more important than ever that we continue to grow ourselves.

I'm certain that Welch would agree that growing yourself is not only the path to leadership, but it's also the job of a leader even after the leadership position is established. After all, Welch spends much of his time developing leaders at the highest levels all over the world. I just wish his famous quote included the idea of lifelong growth.

Here's my unauthorized addition to Welch's classic leadership quote: "Before you are a leader, success is all about growing yourself. When you become a leader, success is all about growing others . . . *while continuing to grow yourself.*"

Okay, so growth shouldn't stop just because one has a leadership position. But how does growth happen effectively? Before answering that question, I think I should issue a warning about fast growth.

NOT ALL GROWTH IS HEALTHY

Too often in our highrise, fast track, modern world (where we get impatient if our download takes more than a few seconds), we mistakenly think that bigger, taller, and faster is better. The ministry world celebrates the "fastest-growing churches" with annual lists and accolades. Leaders of these rapidly growing churches, campus ministries, youth groups, and men's ministries are rewarded with book contracts and keynote speaking slots at national conferences, only to be forgotten and replaced the next year with the newest, fastest-growing ministry leaders.

Because of the misplaced priorities that spring from our microwave-ministry philosophy, pastors of slow-growing churches often suffer from "growth envy" discouragement and are tempted to reject healthy, but slow, methods of growth. Instead, they replace slow methods with the latest get-big-quick growth scheme. Every time I see one of those "fastest-growing church" lists, I want to warn leaders that abnormally rapid and huge growth is often an indication that something is wrong.

Here's an example of how both fast and huge growth can actually be unhealthy.

Anna Swan weighed eighteen pounds at her birth in 1846. By her seventeenth birthday, she stood seven feet eleven inches tall and was working at P. T. Barnum's New York Museum. Eventually, Anna met and fell in love with "Kentucky Giant" Martin Van Buren Bates, who was seven feet nine inches tall. The world's tallest couple was married in 1871. Martin and Anna's daughter was born a year later and, like her mother, weighed eighteen pounds at birth. Unfortunately, their daughter didn't survive birth. Seven years later, Anna gave birth to a twenty-two-pound son who died eleven hours later. Anna died in 1888 at the relatively young age of forty-one.

Serious health disorders are not uncommon in humans who grow abnormally large. Rapid and enormous growth is often caused by a tumor on the gland that controls our development, and results in multiple health problems, including high blood pressure, diabetes, enlargement of the heart, and sometimes, premature death.

Many churches and ministries are like Anna and her babies: they grow fast and large but are actually unhealthy.

I'm not suggesting that all ministry growth is unhealthy. But unusually fast growth often is.

Spiritual health problems also occur when individuals grow into leadership positions too fast. My friend Joey Bonifacio constantly warns pastors against trying to speed up the discipleship process by using the "slow is fast" principle. I think "slow is fast" also applies to leadership development. Most growing organizations need more leaders immediately, but if our goal is strong and healthy leaders, we must slow down the process and resist the temptation to fast track our leadership training.

If you're looking for a quick fix for your leadership needs, this is the wrong book. But if you want a lifelong leadership strategy for yourself and for multiplying your future leaders, keep reading.

The rest of this chapter will focus on four foundational areas that are required for anyone who wants to grow like a leader: calling, compassion, communication, and character.

CALLING

If the starting point for spiritual leadership is a call from God, then church and ministry leaders must continually grow in their understanding of their calling. Since no two individuals are exactly alike, no two callings are exactly alike. However, many human responses to the divine call are eerily similar in that they all seem to offer the same tired excuses.

Consider some of the unique callings and common excuses that are recorded in the Bible.

- **Moses.** Most of us have never had a conversation with a burning bush that could speak, but that's exactly how

God chose to call Moses to deliver His people from slavery. Moses responded with a long list of excuses about why God had picked the wrong man. His excuses included the usual suspects:

- I'm not a leader. (Exodus 3:11)
- I don't know enough about God. (Exodus 3:13)
- They probably won't listen to me. (Exodus 4:1)
- I'm not a good speaker. (Exodus 4:10)

Believe it or not, none of these brilliant excuses succeeded in changing God's mind. Your excuses will probably be equally ineffective.

- **Gideon.** After the death of Joshua, the people of Israel went through cycle after cycle of apostasy, judgment, repentance, and deliverance. The deliverance part of the cycle occurred every time God called a "judge" to preach repentance and break the cycle of apostasy and idolatry. Timid Gideon was the least likely candidate to be a leader, yet God sent an angel to call him out of hiding to the front lines. Gideon responded like many people do when faced with the call of God—he made excuses:

  - If God is good, why is evil happening? (Judges 6:13)
  - But I'm from a poor family. (Judges 6:15)
  - I need a sign. (Judges 6:17)

  As with Moses, none of these excuses caused God to reconsider His original plan for Gideon.

- **Jeremiah.** Years of immoral and idolatrous leadership led to the Babylonian captivity. As usual, in the middle of a season of spiritual and political darkness, God placed His divine call on a future leader. When I say future leader, I mean future to the extreme. Jeremiah was called before he was even born. "Before I formed you in the womb I knew you, and before you were born I consecrated you; I appointed you a prophet to the nations" (Jeremiah 1:5). Jeremiah's prenatal calling was confirmed by a word from God when he was a teenager. And like Moses and Gideon before him, Jeremiah had a pitiful list of unoriginal excuses:

- I don't know how to speak. (Jeremiah 1:6–7)
- I'm too young. (Jeremiah 1:6–7)
- I'm afraid. (Jeremiah 1:8)

I love God's response to Jeremiah's lame excuses: "Behold, I have put my words in your mouth. See, I have set you this day over nations and over kingdoms, to pluck up and to break down, to destroy and to overthrow, to build and to plant" (Jeremiah 1:9–10). Jeremiah's excuses did not negate God's call for him to be a prophet to the nations, and guess what? Your excuses and weaknesses do not negate His call on your life either.

Let me take a moment and attempt to demystify the idea of divine calling. Most of us have never seen a burning bush that did not burn up, and most of us have never heard God talk to us through a bush. Yet many times, we are pretty sure God has called us to do something. I know a few people, but not many, who have had a conversation with a real angel concerning God's calling on their lives. The most well-known callings in the Bible, like the three mentioned above, often involve unusual and supernatural encounters. However, thousands of genuinely called men and women in the Bible and in our churches have never experienced anything out of the ordinary.

AN AUDIBLE VOICE CALLED ME TO MANILA

I hope my story does not cause anyone to experience calling envy, but I was called to the Philippines by an audible voice. I'll never forget hearing and answering that call the first week of May in 1984. It changed my life.

It was over three decades ago, but here's how I remember it. I was in my small apartment in Starkville, Mississippi, where Deborah and I were campus missionaries serving the students of Mississippi State University. It was a Monday night, at around eight o'clock. My phone rang, and I answered the call.

It was then that I clearly and distinctly heard the audible voice of my friend Rice Broocks inviting me to accompany him on a one-month summer mission trip to Manila's University Belt. I asked him a few details about the dates and the cost and told him that if God provided the money, then he could count on Deborah and me being there.

I didn't fast or even pray about it. Rice needed help, and Jesus had already clearly called all His disciples to "Go therefore and make disciples of all nations" (Matthew 28:19). So that was enough for us.

I called a few friends and asked if they would help us. They responded generously, so Deborah and I flew to the Philippines with Rice and our clueless summer mission team. As you know, we stayed, started a church, and I was honored to serve as its senior pastor for over two decades. I still get to serve as part of the apostolic team that oversees Victory Manila and more than seventy Victory churches all over the Philippine Islands.

Deborah and I went to the Philippines because a friend called to ask for help with a summer mission trip. We stayed when everyone else went home because God called us.

Here's how we knew God called us to stay. It wasn't through an audible voice, a burning bush, an angel, or anything unusual or supernatural. After two weeks in the Philippines, during a communion service at the Admiral Hotel on Manila's Roxas Boulevard, my heart was moved with compassion for Manila's university students. And since there wasn't a long line of people willing to stay behind to help, I volunteered. How did I know we were called to stay? I don't know how to explain it; I just knew.

A talking bush, an angelic visitation, a dream, or something else supernatural might have helped me convince Deborah that this was God's will for us, but none of that happened. What I knew in an instant took her a bit longer to recognize as God's calling. In the meantime, she simply trusted me, and God.

Here's the point. Whether you have a dramatic and mystical encounter, complete with voices and visions, or a mundane and not-so-supernatural burden for a campus or city, both can be valid calls from God. For me, the need is usually the call.

COMPASSION

"People don't care how much you know, until they know how much you care." I'm not sure who first said this famous quote, but I agree with it. Anyone who wants to grow like a leader will have to grow in compassion toward people.

I remember a disturbing conversation a few years ago with a pastor who was a great teacher, leading a relatively large congregation. I think he was trying to be funny when he said, "I love everything about ministry, except the people." Most of us who knew him knew that, even if he was joking, he was actually telling the truth. It was obvious that this guy loved to study and teach, but he did not love the people who listened to his teaching. It's no surprise that today, his audience is vastly smaller than when I first heard his amazing teaching. The people no longer care what he knows because they know that he doesn't care.

Jesus was the opposite of this pastor. He not only taught people, He actually cared about them. The Bible records many stories about His love and compassion, including this one.

Jesus' cousin and close friend, John the Baptist, was unjustly imprisoned, then brutally murdered by Herod. Being fully human and fully divine, Jesus responded like any man would respond when a dear friend dies: "Now when Jesus heard this, he withdrew from there in a boat to a desolate place by himself. But when the crowds heard it, they followed him on foot from the towns" (Matthew 14:13).

Jesus wanted to be alone to grieve the loss of His cousin. But, as always, the crowds wanted something from Him. I would have sent them away for another day. But that's not what Jesus did. "When he went ashore he saw a great crowd, and he had compassion on them and healed their sick" (Matthew 14:14). Compassion empowered Jesus to minister to the crowds, even when He was physically and emotionally exhausted.

After Jesus healed the huge crowds, the disciples pleaded with Him to send them all away. But instead of sending them home, Jesus told His disciples to feed them.

Compassion heals and feeds. It also opens our eyes to see beyond the obvious.

A few chapters before this, Matthew narrates another time Jesus was moved by compassion. "When he saw the crowds, he had compassion for them, because they were harassed and helpless, like sheep without a shepherd" (Matthew 9:36).

Compassion enabled Jesus to see not just a crowd of people, but individuals who were "harassed and helpless, like sheep without a shepherd." When our eyes are opened and we see people as they really are, we will realize when they need help. Compassion will enable us to actually help them with the gospel, rather than fearing, hating, or rejecting them.

Earlier in this chapter, I mentioned that morning in the Admiral Hotel when I knew I was called to Manila. It was one of those moments when compassion opened blind eyes and softened a hard heart. For two weeks, I had seen and preached to crowds of Filipino students. That morning, compassion changed the way I saw the crowds. I now saw real people who were "harassed and helpless, like sheep without a shepherd," and I had to do something about it. I couldn't just return to the status quo in America. So I stayed.

Leaders, no matter where they are on the leadership journey, must grow in their understanding of calling and in their ability to extend compassion to hurting people. Responding to God's calling and having a heart of compassion toward people forces leaders to grow and upgrade their ability to communicate God's message.

COMMUNICATION

Moses instinctively knew that his calling would require him to communicate God's word to His people and their Egyptian captors. As I mentioned earlier, like many of us, Moses felt wholly inadequate as a communicator. "Oh, my Lord, I am not eloquent, either in the past or since you have spoken to your servant, but I am slow of speech and of tongue" (Exodus 4:10). Jeremiah also knew that his calling would require communication skills that would have to be upgraded. "Ah, Lord God! Behold, I do not know how to speak, for I am only a youth" (Jeremiah 1:6).

Speaking of not being eloquent and not knowing how to speak in public, I'll never forget my first public speech (although it was extremely forgettable to everyone else). It was the summer of 1971. I was twelve years old. The Little League Baseball season was over, and it was time for the awards banquet. The morning of our team banquet, my dad (who was also our team coach) asked me to give a brief after-dinner speech on behalf of the team. I was so terrified, I hardly ate that night.

The flow of a Little League team banquet goes like this. First, the twelve players and their parents eat. Then the coach says something nice and encouraging about each player. Then the designated player/spokesman gives a response—basically a "thank you" to the coaches and parents. As of that morning, I was our designated team spokesman.

My speech contained exactly eight words and lasted less than five seconds. I had planned to say more than eight words, but I froze.

Here's what I said. "I just want to thank the coaches, and . . ."

If my speech had been seven words rather than eight, it would have simply been the shortest speech in Little League Baseball banquet history. But ending a speech with the word "and" implies that something else will be said. That eighth word was the problem, and I could not get it back in my mouth.

As soon as I uttered the word "and," my brain quit functioning. Apparently, my extreme nervousness and terror brought on a case of temporary adolescent Alzheimer's. I could not remember what I was supposed to say next, so I stood there, and said nothing. As this long awkward silence engulfed the room and the whole Little League season, I wanted to disappear. But that didn't happen, so I eventually sat down, and made an inward vow to never again give a speech.

But God's call on my life required that I break my childhood vow of silence. It also required that I learn how to communicate in a variety of ways, including the following.

1. **Teaching and preaching.** Some people are natural-born speakers, but preaching and teaching did not come naturally to me. It's obvious from the embarrassing story above that I possess no natural public-speaking talent. I'm more of a natural-born listener and observer. In my family, I was the shy one. Whatever speaking, teaching, and preaching skills I have are acquired skills, not mystical gifts that magically appeared in my life.

For me, learning to speak in public required discipline, practice, and feedback. I knew this area of my life needed to develop if I was to be the leader God called me to be, so I did everything in my ability to grow and become a better speaker. After over thirty-five years as a pastor and teacher, I'm still learning and changing, and hopefully getting better.

As a leader, I realized that I not only needed to grow in my Sunday preaching skills, I also needed to upgrade my ability to communicate in a small-group discipleship setting. The communication skills that work with crowds of hundreds and thousands don't work so well in small discipleship groups at coffee shops. And it requires a completely different set of communication skills to lead a ministry board meeting, a church staff meeting, or a global Skype call. You may be a great preacher or teacher, but those skills are usually counterproductive in other leadership settings. Leaders must grow in every area of spoken communication, not just preaching and teaching.

2. Writing and blogging. Developing effective speaking skills is simply the starting point for spiritual leaders. Church and campus ministry leaders also need to acquire, develop, and upgrade their writing skills. Three decades ago, when our church first went multisite, we started a monthly publication called *Victory Fire* in order to communicate our mission, vision, and values to Victory members who rarely saw me face-to-face. Committing to a monthly column forced me to grow in my writing ability. Years later, when the Internet became more popular, we replaced the monthly magazine with a website that included my monthly column in a then-new format called a blog. Eventually, my monthly column became a weekly blog. And eventually, my job and my team demanded that I write some books.

3. Twitter and Instagram. I resisted (mocked) all forms of social media for several years, until the communications people in my office finally forced me to get on Multiply, the now-defunct predecessor of Facebook. (Anyone out there remember Multiply?) As soon as I saw the global communications capability of social media, I was hooked. Multiply actually made the task of keeping in touch with hundreds of leaders from dozens of nations possible. And it was all done in real time. By the time Multiply died, I was already on Twitter and saw no need for Facebook. One social media account was enough for me. But again, my office prevailed and soon, I was communicating through Facebook as well. Somewhere along the way, while I was not looking, the Manila communications team moved my blogs from Multiply and Facebook to a new and improved website. I was told to use my Twitter account to drive traffic to my dotcom. And now, I'm on Instagram.

Here's the point. As church and ministry leaders, we have a message from God that demands we leverage every channel to get that message to the right people. Notice that I didn't say we should get our message to as many people as possible. Leaders should be more concerned with getting their message to the right people than to the most people. I'm thankful for a team of brilliant communications specialists who push me to the appropriate medium to get the message to the right people. I certainly haven't mastered any of them, but I'm committed to continuous growth in my communication skills.

No matter who or where you're called to lead, your leadership calling will require that your communication skills constantly grow. Growing not only means getting better at speaking or writing, but also acquiring skills that are way outside of your comfort zone.

CHARACTER

While it's vital for leaders to continually grow in their calling, compassion for people, and communication skills, the most important and foundational aspect of growing like a leader is to grow in character. If our character is growing, everything else needed for effective leadership will grow accordingly. And if certain leadership essentials are lagging behind, character growth will usually make up for whatever else is missing.

Paul knew that fulfilling a calling was dependent on developing character. When exhorting his friends in Ephesus to "walk in a manner worthy of the calling," notice that Paul did not give them theological education standards or a ministry to-do list. Instead, he gave them a character list.

> I therefore, a prisoner for the Lord, urge you to walk in a manner worthy of the calling to which you have been called, with all humility and gentleness, with patience, bearing with one another in love, eager to maintain the unity of the Spirit in the bond of peace. (Ephesians 4:1–3)

In other words, if you want to fulfill your calling, you will need some character upgrades including, but not limited to, humility, gentleness, love, unity, and peace.

RELATIONAL CHARACTER TRAITS

It doesn't require deep study to notice that most of the character qualities mentioned by Paul are relational. Since we lead people, we must focus on developing the type of character that upgrades our relational skills. It's tragic for ministry leaders to have highly developed organizational leadership skills, but dysfunctional relational skills. Learning the skills necessary to lead meetings and organizations is relatively easy. In contrast, leading people is much more complex. Meetings and organizations don't get offended. But people tend to have feelings, get hurt, and react. I guess that's why the preacher friend I mentioned earlier loved everything about ministry but the people.

The New Testament gives us multiple lists of Christian character traits required of all leaders. These lists have a lot of overlap, but the one thing that stands out is the emphasis on character traits that make a positive impact on relationships. Notice the relational words in the following passage:

> This is why I left you in Crete, so that you might put what remained into order, and appoint elders in every town as I directed you—if anyone is above reproach, the husband of one wife, and his children are believers and not open to the charge of debauchery or insubordination. For an overseer, as God's steward, must be above reproach. He must not be arrogant or quick-tempered or a drunkard or violent or greedy for gain, but hospitable, a lover of good, self-controlled, upright, holy, and disciplined. He must hold firm to the trustworthy word as taught, so that he may be able to give instruction in sound doctrine and also to rebuke those who contradict it. (Titus 1:5–9)

Paul's instruction to Titus with regard to qualifications for elders relied heavily on character traits that were connected to relational leadership. He gives a similar list of relational character traits to help Timothy appoint elders and deacons in Ephesus.

> Therefore an overseer must be above reproach, the husband of one wife, sober-minded, self-controlled, respectable, hospitable, able to teach, not a drunkard, not violent but gentle, not quarrelsome, not a lover of money. He must manage his own household well, with all dignity keeping his children submissive, for if someone does not know how to manage his own household, how will he care for God's church? He must not be a recent convert, or he may become puffed up with conceit and fall into the condemnation of the devil. Moreover, he must be well thought of by outsiders, so

that he may not fall into disgrace, into a snare of the devil. (1 Timothy 3:2–7)

Paul also required relational character from his deacons.

Deacons likewise must be dignified, not double-tongued, not addicted to much wine, not greedy for dishonest gain. They must hold the mystery of the faith with a clear conscience. And let them also be tested first; then let them serve as deacons if they prove themselves blameless. Their wives likewise must be dignified, not slanderers, but sober-minded, faithful in all things. Let deacons each be the husband of one wife, managing their children and their own households well. (1 Timothy 3:8–12)

Notice that it wasn't random relational character traits that qualified or disqualified a person for local church leaders. Paul placed an emphasis specifically on family relationships. Spiritual leadership is supposed to start at home.

HOW IS CHARACTER DEVELOPED?

Leadership gifts are deposited in an instant. Godly character is developed over a lifetime. But how does character development happen?

A quick look at the New Testament Greek word for "character" points us to the act of engraving. It refers to an engraving tool, and is used in the context of cutting, carving, or making an impression. And finally, it can mean a stamp or the act of stamping in order to reproduce an image on a coin or other material. This ancient stamping process required pressure.

But we don't even need to look at the New Testament Greek word in order to understand character. The modern

English definition of character is essentially the same as the ancient Greek. *Webster's Dictionary* uses the following words and phrases to define character when used as a noun: a distinctive mark, a letter or symbol, a peculiar quality or the sum of qualities. When character is a verb, *Webster's* defines character with words like: to engrave, to inscribe, to distinguish.

So character is a distinctive mark or stamp that is carved or impressed on a person through cutting, chiseling, or pressure through an external and/or an internal force.

For the Christian leader, that external and/or internal force that forms character is God. Two New Testament passages describe the process God uses to stamp His character on us: "... we rejoice in our sufferings, knowing that suffering produces endurance, and endurance produces character, and character produces hope ..." (Romans 5:3–4).

Paul says that in order to have character, we must first experience and rejoice in suffering. If we avoid suffering or if we complain our way through suffering, then character is not produced.

James makes basically the same point about character development.

> Count it all joy, my brothers, when you meet trials of various kinds, for you know that the testing of your faith produces steadfastness. And let steadfastness have its full effect, that you may be perfect and complete, lacking in nothing. (James 1:2–4)

In other words, if we want to be "complete" and "lacking in nothing," then we will need to endure trials and testing. If we avoid trials and tests, then we will not be complete and lacking in nothing.

PAUL:	Trials Tests	**>**	**Steadfastness**	**>**	**Perfect Complete**
JAMES:	Suffering	**>**	**Endurance**	**>**	**Character**

Here's a verse from the Old Testament that describes the same character-development process that Paul and James teach: "The crucible is for silver, and the furnace is for gold, and the Lord tests hearts" (Proverbs 17:3). Gold and silver are purified by intense heat that causes hidden impurities to rise to the top so they can be exposed and removed. In the same way, God tests our hearts by heating up the circumstances in our lives. These tests cause hidden impurities and ungodly attitudes to rise to the top so they can be exposed and removed.

Notice that it is God who tests the heart. When we have a providential perspective of life, we accept that what may seem like random, difficult, or unfair situations are, in reality, God orchestrating life in order to test and purify our hearts. This perspective makes life's tough times have meaning and value. So next time temporal things are externally falling apart, realize that God is doing something internal and eternal. He's testing your heart and forming your character.

Today, it's common for church leaders to be known for their ministry accomplishments, communication skills, and the size of their churches. In contrast, the Bible described Job as a man who was "blameless and upright, one who feared God and turned away from evil" (Job 1:1). This passage identifies and describes Job in terms of his internal character, with no reference to his temporal accomplishments. When a person has godly character, accomplishments are inevitable and do not even need to be listed. We can assume the accomplishments are there. And when character is developed, other areas of ministry growth (understanding calling, extending compassion, and upgrading communication skills) will happen in a healthy manner.

Once we learn to grow like a leader, the next step is to multiply like a leader.

DISCUSSION QUESTIONS X

1. What has God called you to do? Where has God called you to serve? Who has God called you to walk with?
2. How do you usually respond to trials and suffering? How should you respond to trials and suffering?
3. What is the most difficult trial and testing of your faith you have experienced?

5

HOW TO MULTIPLY LIKE A LEADER

There's never been a multiplication movement that was not committed deeply to disciple-making.
ALAN HIRSCH, Missiologist

Every pastor will either reproduce himself digitally on a screen or incarnationally in the life of a disciple.
JIM LAFFOON, Prophet

. . . what you have heard from me in the presence of many witnesses entrust to faithful men who will be able to teach others also.
2 TIMOTHY 2:2

I n the late eighties, when I was a young, struggling cross-cultural church planter, I attended a church-growth conference at Yoido Full Gospel Church in Seoul, Korea. In those days, pastors from all over the world flocked to Korea to learn from Dr. Cho and his team at Yoido, which happened to be the largest church in the world with over 500,000 members.

The conference I attended included 700 pastors from thirty nations. I don't remember any of the teachings, but I do remember returning to Manila with a bigger vision, stronger faith, and a renewed determination to make an impact on my whole city with the gospel.

Victory Manila is not even close to the size of Yoido Full Gospel Church. But every year, more and more pastors from around the world visit us to observe, learn, and ask questions about building a healthy discipleship culture and leading a growing disciple-making church.

We do our best to host and help every church planter and pastor who visits. Over the years, I've noticed that visiting pastors often make the same three observations and comments about Victory Manila. Here's what they observe and mention about our church: we have lots of committed men, young people, and strong leaders.

These three observations get the attention of visitors because most churches in the Philippines have a disproportionate number of female members. But Victory's male and female numbers are almost equal. Secondly, because we emphasize campus ministry, we have thousands of vibrant young people. And finally, almost everyone who visits Victory notices and asks about leadership. They want to know the secret to finding, recruiting, hiring, and keeping a deep bench of strong leaders. As I've already mentioned, we didn't find, recruit, or hire our leaders. We built them from the ground up.

The rest of this chapter will explain how we built a leadership-multiplication culture at Victory Manila, how we lost it, and how we recovered it.

A SERIOUS LEADERSHIP SHORTAGE

On September 8, 2011, I walked into the Acacia Hotel function room in Alabang, just south of Manila, to meet with two dozen Victory leaders. The purpose of the Alabang meeting was to address our multiplication challenge and to solve our leadership shortage. Looking back, I think it was one of the most significant meetings in the history of our church.

In order to get the most comprehensive wisdom available, we had invited a diverse group of Victory leaders—young, old, male, female, urban, provincial. We had leaders from Victory Manila, the surrounding provinces, our campus ministry, and the School of World Missions. We also had leaders of new congregations of 200 and of older congregations of 10,000. Some had started following Jesus in the 1980s; some were not even born in the 1980s. We had mothers, fathers, newlyweds, and singles.

It was a diverse group, but they were all leaders—leaders who had been equipped and empowered in our church over the previous twenty-seven years.

Our plan was to spend several days prayerfully and honestly discussing what we had done right for our first twenty years and what we had done wrong for the last seven years. This Alabang strategic leadership summit was the much-anticipated and much-needed follow-up to a meeting that had taken place exactly two years earlier in September of 2009 (described in the introduction of this book). That meeting adjusted our thinking and our target, but it did little to solve our ongoing leadership crisis. In fact, in the two years that had passed since then, our leadership needs had grown explosively, along with our church.

Our multiplication challenge was even more urgent in 2011 than it had been in 2009. Since we had first spotted our vast leadership voids in 2009, Victory Manila grew from 37,200 to over 48,000 in weekend attendance. That's almost 11,000 new people in twenty-four months. During that same time, we had remained relatively stagnant in small-group growth—remaining at around 3,500 Victory groups. Our ratio of weekend worship attendees to small-group leaders had risen from roughly ten to one in 2009 to thirteen to one in 2011. Keep in mind that it had been steadily getting worse every year since 2004, when the ratio had been a healthy five to one.

The outcome objective of our meeting was simple: to find the problem and fix our leadership-development strategy—fast.

As I mentioned earlier, the lack of small-group leaders was just the tip of the iceberg. We had leadership shortages in virtually every department of our church. The only area where leadership development seemed to be keeping pace with our growth was in the training of preachers—an area we had intentionally focused on as we began multiplying congregations and worship services in the early 2000s.

As of this writing, Victory Manila has 137 weekly worship services in twenty-five locations. Because I feel called to make disciples and train leaders, I have never been comfortable playing video sermons or doing live sermon video feeds. I have no problem with churches that do video campuses, but I can't because it would undermine my calling to equip and empower Filipino leaders.

All 137 Victory Manila worship services have live preachers. Since the typical Victory pastor only preaches two services a weekend, we feature sixty-five preachers every weekend, all preaching the same topic and text.

My friend Jim Laffoon once said, "Every pastor will either reproduce himself digitally on a screen or incarnationally in the life of a disciple." Reproducing myself in live preachers is a lot messier than broadcasting sermons on screens. But in spite of the messes that we sometimes have to clean up, I am glad that God called Victory Manila to multiply this way.

You can see why we invested a lot of time, money, and energy into training Filipino preachers. Unfortunately, we didn't invest nearly enough time, money, and energy into training leaders for all the other areas of our church. We were desperately playing catch-up and the clock was ticking.

BACK TO THE FUTURE

We had developed dozens of strong leaders in our church over the years, so clearly we had done something right for several decades. We realized that maybe the question wasn't really what we were doing wrong as much as it was a question of what we had done right in our past, but had inadvertently stopped doing in recent years.

Many times, my thoughts went back to the early days of our church, back to the day when I wrote our first mission statement.

In 1984, our three-week-old church was meeting in the basement of the Tandem Cinema on Recto Avenue in Manila. I was sitting in my University Belt office (Dunkin' Donuts), and I scribbled something on a napkin that would shape the direction of our church for decades to come: *We exist to honor God and advance His kingdom by making disciples, training leaders, and taking dominion.*

Over the years, our mission statement had remained basically the same, undergoing only a few changes. Most significantly, in the late eighties we changed "taking dominion" to "planting churches"—signifying an attempt to clarify core initiatives and a conscious disassociation with the lunatic fringe of Dominion Theology.

From the beginning, even before that slight edit in our mission statement, Victory was obsessively focused on making disciples, training leaders, and planting churches. And, as the years passed, we got better and better at all three. Each year, we made more disciples, trained more leaders, and planted more churches in Manila, the Philippines, Asia, and the rest of the world.

As I thought about the importance of our mission statement in setting the direction of our church since 1984, my memory moved ahead to the next major change in our mission statement.

In 2007, in the middle of a general rebranding effort and in a specific effort to place a laser focus on making disciples, we stripped down our original mission statement, *To honor God and advance His kingdom by making disciples, training leaders, and planting churches,* to just four words: *Honor God. Make Disciples.*

Today, those four words seem obvious. Not so much then. I remember rigorous debate about whether Victory's core message and calling was to make disciples or train leaders. Finally, after much discussion, debate, and prayer, the team agreed that if we didn't make disciples, we wouldn't be able to train leaders. In the Victory version of "the chicken or the egg" debate, we decided that making disciples had to be first and foremost.

The clincher for us was that Jesus called His followers to go and make disciples. I'm sure He also wanted them to equip and empower leaders, but since Jesus emphasized discipleship, we took that as our cue. Missiologist Alan Hirsch seems to agree with Jesus (and with us) that disciple-making is core: "There's never been a multiplication movement that was not committed deeply to disciple-making." If anyone was to be committed deeply to discipleship, we were determined it would be us.

Around this same time, Rice Broocks, my friend and Every Nation cofounder, was speaking along with me at a conference for pastors and church leaders. During a Q & A session, Rice and I were asked to make a presentation about Every Nation Leadership Institute (ENLI), which was our primary means for leadership instruction at Victory Manila for many years. After presenting the need for theological education and practical ministry training, Rice asked me a rhetorical question to make a point to our audience about the importance of ENLI. "Steve, would you say that our Every Nation Leadership Institute is the key ingredient that has enabled you and your team to raise up so many great Filipino leaders at Victory?"

Rice was shocked when I answered, "No."

He rephrased the question, and again, I answered, "No. Rice, as important as ENLI is, leadership training is not the key." After a short pause for effect, I continued. "Discipleship is the key. If potential leaders enter ENLI with strong, healthy discipleship foundations, our graduates have the potential to become great leaders. But if people enroll in ENLI with shaky foundations and no discipleship, then no matter how good the curriculum and no matter how good the teachers, ENLI will not produce leaders."

Rice agreed, and we continued our leadership talk.

MAKING DISCIPLES IS NOT ENOUGH

The rationale behind the change to our four-word mission statement was simple. We were trying to sharpen our focus so that if someone were to ask the question, "What is the one thing that you do as an organization?" our answer would be the same every time—*make disciples*. As a leadership team in 2007, we discussed the changes in our mission statement extensively, and we all agreed that this was the way to go. We wanted to master one move (making disciples). We wanted to identify what we could be the best at (making disciples). We wanted to identify what was foundational to everything else God called us to do (making disciples).

Armed with the new shortened version of our mission—"Honor God. Make disciples."—we did just that. We set out to honor God and make disciples with reckless abandon. We strategically stopped everything that did not directly contribute to disciple-making.

Looking back, I think it was the right move.

But I also think that shortening our mission statement may have caused us to slow down our aggressive leadership training. Our focus shifted more and more on making disciples and away from leadership development. We didn't stop all leadership development, but we definitely dialed it back a bit. We didn't intend to stop training leaders, but training leaders lost its visibility and priority in our church. We assumed that if we focused on making disciples, leaders would automatically emerge.

It was a false assumption. Leadership development doesn't happen organically; it happens strategically and intentionally.

As we discussed what had happened since our 2007 mission statement edits, we realized that all leaders are disciples—but not all disciples are leaders. In other words, discipleship is the vital foundation for leadership, but leadership development must still be intentional. If someone is a faithful disciple, they have the potential to become a leader, but that potential still needs to be developed.

As I and other Victory old-timers shared these thoughts at our Alabang leadership meeting, we all realized the simple, yet painful truth—we had massive leadership shortages because we were less aggressive, less intentional, and less strategic about training leaders than we had been before. The problem wasn't necessarily that we had dropped "training leaders" from our mission statement but, rather, that we had dropped it from the top line of our list of priorities.

We had figured out the problem. Now we had to fix it.

REVERSE-ENGINEERING THE LEADERSHIP STRATEGY

"What factors contributed to your leadership development at Victory?"

This question was being discussed at every table in the meeting. We had a room full of amazing leaders who had been trained in our church for over two decades. We needed their insight to figure out what we had done right.

We needed to create a new strategy for leadership development, but we didn't need to reinvent the wheel. We wanted to rediscover what had worked in the past and make sure we either continued or resurrected that leadership-development strategy with greater intentionality and focus.

Our goal was simple—*to reverse-engineer the Victory leadership culture.*

What had we done to get all these amazing leaders, and how could we capture the various leadership-development components into a coherent and repeatable strategy?

The discussion at my table began with stories and memories of the early days of our ministry and one of our early attempts to intentionally train leaders—our summer intensive "Leadership Lab." People told stories of times when a pastor or friend challenged them to step up to leadership. As the leaders discussed this question at their tables, markers and large pieces of colored paper were passed out to each group. The purpose was to capture some of the common themes or ideas discussed.

When we finished our discussion, each group taped their papers on a large wall in the meeting room and explained how what was written on their paper had contributed to their leadership development. As we stepped back and looked at the collage of colored paper on the wall, we recognized some common themes. We began moving the papers around into clusters based on these themes. Some papers were put in one cluster then moved to another. Others were put in between clusters.

After some discussion, we observed four broad categories: God, formal training, relationships, and an empowering culture.

Obviously these categories needed some refinement and explanation.

Papers that we had clustered under the "God" category said things like: "sense of calling," "natural gifts and talents," "circumstances," and "prophetic words." Basically, many people felt that, while their leadership development was influenced by a variety of factors, their calling to leadership and ministry began with God. He had wired them to lead. He had called them. And He had made it clear—whether through godly counsel, an inner sense from the Holy Spirit, or circumstances.

Papers that we had clustered under "formal training" said things like: "Leadership Lab," "Victory Leadership Institute," "seminars from outside speakers," "seminary classes," "missions conferences," and "John Maxwell books and cassette tapes." In short, this category captured intentional information transfer that had helped the individual grow as a leader—whether it was in a classroom or by directed self-study.

Papers that we had clustered under "relationships" said things like: "small-group leader's encouragement to lead," "conversations with my pastor," "trust from senior leadership," and "healthy correction from leaders." This category was full of papers that emphasized the value of having people in their life to encourage them to lead, correct them when they messed up, and help them identify their gifts and passion.

Papers that we had clustered under "an empowering culture" said things like: "I was first asked to preach when I was sixteen" and "pastor trusted me." Many comments expressed shock, surprise, and honor that they were allowed to actually participate in significant ministry leadership, despite their inexperience.

We figured out what had worked in the past. Now we needed to figure out how to create a transferable strategy—that incorporated these four categories we had observed—to solve our leadership shortage.

LEADERSHIP DEVELOPMENT: INTENTIONAL OR ORGANIC?

If you're uncomfortable with the idea of an intentional leadership-development strategy, you might want to ask yourself why. It sounds very spiritual to say that we're just going to make disciples and leadership development will take care of itself organically (whatever that means). The problem is that organic, non-intentional leadership development, like unicorns and Santa Claus, only exists in an imaginary world.

Discipleship is the obvious starting point of spiritual leadership. Disciples are the raw material out of which we can shape leaders. Our primary objective is to make disciples—to help people follow Jesus, fish for people, and fellowship with other believers. But if we stop there—if we intentionally make disciples and don't intentionally identify and train leaders—then we will have two problems: one present problem and one future problem.

Present problem: if we don't train leaders, our growth will either plateau or it will crush our current leaders. Healthy discipleship growth will always threaten to overwhelm current leaders and leadership structures. The only way to solve this problem is to either stop growing or train and empower new leaders. Doing something to deliberately stop God-given growth is not an option. So really, there's only one viable solution to this multiplication challenge: accelerate the equipping and empowering of new leaders.

Future problem: if we don't constantly train new leaders, we won't experience multi-generational growth. Being one-generation wonders is not a viable option. Throughout the Bible, God often identified Himself as multi-generational.

For example, He is the God of Abraham, Isaac, and Jacob. Three generations of continuity.

The Apostle Paul showed a serious commitment to training and empowering future leaders in both his writings and his lifestyle—always bringing young leaders along with him on his missionary journeys. Perhaps Paul's most well-known disciple was Timothy, a young man from Lystra who traveled with him extensively and eventually became the leader of the church in Ephesus.

Compared to his bold and fearless mentor, Timothy seemed to be too timid to be a great leader, plus he had some serious recurring fear issues. But rather than disqualifying him from potential leadership, Timothy's fear and timidity struggles underscored the importance of intentional leadership development and personal mentoring. To help Timothy overcome his natural timidity, Paul reminded him that "the Spirit God gave us does not make us timid, but gives us power, love and self-discipline" (2 Timothy 1:7, NIV). Paul also recruited others to help Timothy break the stronghold of fear. He told the church at Corinth, "When Timothy comes, see to it that he has nothing to fear while he is with you" (1 Corinthians 16:10, NIV).

Part of Timothy's leadership development happened as he accompanied Paul on missionary trips. When we first meet Timothy in Lystra (Acts 16), he is described as "a disciple" with a Jewish mother and a Greek father. At that point, he was not a leader; he was simply a disciple. That's the starting point of all biblical leadership.

The next thing we know, young Timothy is traveling with Paul all over the world on church-planting mission trips. They ministered in Phrygia, Galatia, and Mysia. When they attempted to preach in Bithynia, "the Spirit of Jesus did not allow them" (Acts 16:7). So they proceeded to Troas, where Paul had his famous "Macedonian Call." And, of course, they set out for Macedonia. Imagine the leadership lessons Timothy learned as he traveled with Paul week after week on all those missions. I'm sure Paul appreciated Timothy's company, but I think the main point was to upgrade Timothy's leadership through a mobile, frontline internship.

Occasionally Paul left Timothy behind, on his own, to help a church. Again, this played an important part in Timothy's leadership development.

While Paul's mentoring of Timothy was more hands-on and informal, his mentorship style was not the only biblical method of leadership development. Samuel had a "school of the prophets" that probably combined formal teaching with informal mentoring. Elijah and Elisha equipped and empowered their "sons of the prophets," a group of ministers that certainly came about intentionally, rather than accidentally or organically. And Jesus didn't leave leadership multiplication to chance. He used a variety of methods to form twelve average, provincial young men into some of the greatest leaders of their time.

Here's the point: intentional leadership development is not unspiritual. It's actually extremely spiritual, biblical, and essential.

REDISCOVERING LEADERSHIP DEVELOPMENT: THE FOUR LEADERSHIP MULTIPLIERS

Back to our 2011 meeting in Alabang. After intense discussion, we had four broad categories of leadership catalysts pasted on the walls. Our next job was to make some sense of all the information we had gathered.

As we looked at the walls covered with colored paper that was sorted into four categories, we weren't sure what to do next. Every leader in the room recognized that their leadership development had been influenced by a combination of all four categories. Clearly, we had a strategy that worked—we just didn't realize it. Our task was to make it memorable, duplicable, and transferable.

Our discussion moved toward creating a strategy that was easy to remember. We wanted something like the Four Es our church used for making disciples: *engage, establish, equip,* and *empower.*

God, formal training, relationship, and an empowering culture didn't quite have the same ring to it. Several joking stabs at alliteration were made, but nothing really stuck until Jun Escosar stood to make his suggestion: "What if we frame the four categories as four principles of leadership development: identification, instruction, impartation, and internship?"

Shocked that someone had managed to use alliteration and make sense at the same time, the noisy room grew silent as we thought about Jun's suggestion. *Identification. Instruction. Impartation. Internship.*

Could it really be that simple and that obvious? Here's how Jun explained his leadership-multiplication strategy suggestion.

- *Identification (God)*—identify potential leaders and help potential leaders identify their God-given gifts, calling, and opportunities to lead

- *Instruction (formal training)*—transfer essential information to the potential leader and give him or her the tools to think like a leader
- *Impartation (relationships)*—shape and strengthen the character of the leader and mentor and encourage him or her in the early stages of leadership
- *Internship (empowering culture)*—give the young leader opportunities to watch, learn, and lead along with more experienced leaders

When Jun finished, we didn't even need a debate. We had rediscovered our long-forgotten leadership-development strategy, and Jun had defined it with words that made it memorable, duplicable, and transferable. We now call them the four leadership multipliers. But we still had a lot of work to do. We needed to figure out how to contextualize this strategy for our current and future church and campus ministry needs.

INSTITUTIONALIZING THE INTUITIVE

When we rediscovered that the Victory leadership-development strategy consisted of four simple, doable parts—identification, instruction, impartation, internship—we were able to rebuild a healthy leadership-multiplication culture.

In the past six years, we seem to have revived Victory's leadership-multiplication strategy and culture. Because of our growth, we still need leaders at every level of our organization, but we're no longer desperately lagging behind with no solution in sight. As soon as we institutionalized the intuitive, our ability to train new leaders started keeping pace with our growth.

The next four chapters will explain the four leadership multipliers—identification, instruction, impartation, and internship—in detail.

DISCUSSION QUESTIONS X

1. Which of the four leadership multipliers (identification, instruction, impartation, internship) do you think would be easiest to put into practice? Why?
2. Which one do you find most challenging? What can you do to address this challenge?
3. Have you viewed leadership development as something strategic or intentional? Why or why not?

DISCOVERING
A LEADERSHIP
STRATEGY

6

IDENTIFICATION

Knowing who you are is the foundation for being great.

SHAWN COREY CARTER (JAY Z), Singer

Who you are is not what you do. Identity is unchanging. Being comes before doing. Who you are determines what you do.

BRAD LOMENICK, Leadership Consultant

For you formed my inward parts; you knitted me together in my mother's womb. I praise you, for I am fearfully and wonderfully made. Wonderful are your works; my soul knows it very well.

PSALM 139:13–14

When we first moved to the Philippines, there was significant civil unrest in Manila as the Marcos regime was losing control of the population—particularly the young people. Each day, anti-government rallies were happening in the streets of Manila's University Belt, which sometimes resulted in violent clashes with the police.

Our new church, which met in the basement of Tandem Cinema in the heart of the U-Belt, sometimes smelled of tear gas as students poured into our evangelistic meetings after marching and protesting on Recto Avenue. Whether they came to our basement church out of genuine interest or just to get out of the chaos on the streets, we welcomed them and took every opportunity to preach the gospel.

In those days, one of our most effective evangelism tools was a multi-media seminar called "Rock and Roll: A Search for God" (or the Rock Seminar for short). By juxtaposing the message of AC/DC, Iron Maiden, Judas Priest, Black Sabbath, and other hardcore rock bands with the message of Jesus, the Rock Seminar presented the gospel in a way that made sense to youth in the rock and roll culture of the eighties.

We held regular Rock Seminars in the Tandem Cinema basement and on every high school and university campus that would allow us. I'm pretty sure this method of presenting the gospel would be irrelevant today, but it was very effective back in the day. If you were to talk to longtime Victory members from the 1980s, many of them would include the Rock Seminar as a turning point in their spiritual journey.

YOUNG INEXPERIENCED LEADERS

One week in 1986, when our church was about eighteen months old, I realized that I had double-booked my schedule and wouldn't be present at an upcoming Rock Seminar. In our staff meeting, we discussed two options: cancel or find a replacement. I didn't want to cancel the event, so I asked if anyone on our young and inexperienced staff would like to lead it—a task that involved reading from a manuscript during a slideshow, giving a short gospel presentation, then following up with new believers afterwards.

When I made the proposal, one hand shot up quickly. Just like a year before (see story in chapter 2), it was a white hand—an American who had joined our team shortly after the original 1984 outreach. He was a veteran minister, so I knew he would do a good job, but I was looking for a Filipino volunteer. My reason for staying in the Philippines wasn't to build a church that would be led by Western missionaries. It was to equip and empower Filipinos to minister and lead.

Ignoring the white hand, I said, "Jun, would you and Ferdie lead the Rock Seminar?"

Jun agreed to take on this last-minute assignment. Ferdie didn't respond at all. He just sat there, frozen. Those who know Jun and Ferdie today would find it difficult to believe that they weren't the first people to volunteer, but many years ago, they weren't quite as confident and bold as they are today.

Jun and Ferdie were two of the first people to attend our initial outreach meetings in 1984. At this point, eighteen months later, they had both graduated and were two of our first Filipino staff members.

Jun had turned down a great job to join our team. I thought he had leadership potential, and I wanted to see how he would respond to unplanned responsibility. So I "volunteered" him to present the Rock Seminar. With just a few days to prepare, Jun eagerly read the seminar manual (so many times that he virtually memorized the presentation). When the day of the seminar arrived, Jun was comforted by the fact that I would not be there to hear it, in case it was a disaster. Plus, Ferdie would be there as his backup.

Far from being a disaster, Jun and Ferdie tag-teamed to lead one of the most successful Rock Seminars ever (based on the number of students who responded to the gospel invitation). Whenever I or another American would lead the seminars, we generally had a handful of people respond positively to the gospel presentation at the end, but sometimes none would. When Jun presented the Rock Seminar and Ferdie followed up with the gospel presentation, nearly the entire room responded in repentance and faith.

In those days, we asked people who responded to the gospel message to fill out blue commitment cards. I'll never forget the moment Jun and Ferdie walked into my office with the thickest stack of blue cards any of us had ever seen. That was the day I retired from Rock Seminar duties. It was also the day that Jun and Ferdie became our official Rock Seminar evangelists.

Looking at the way Jun and Ferdie lead today, one might assume that their 1984 leadership potential was so obvious that delegating ministry responsibility to them was a no-brainer. In reality, picking them to lead was relatively a simple decision, not because their leadership capacity was so huge, but because the pool of potential leaders was so small.

There's one more reason I identified Jun and Ferdie as potential leaders, and it has to do with F.A.I.T.H.

LOOKING FOR F.A.I.T.H.

From the very beginning of our church, we aggressively empowered young, inexperienced leaders to do ministry. Sometimes it worked beautifully, as in the above example, and other times, there were problems. To protect the guilty, I won't mention any of the many disaster stories.

At first, I wasn't sure exactly what I was looking for when I identified potential ministers and leaders. Sometimes, people were chosen simply because I remembered their names and I forgot the other person's name. Sometimes, the person sitting closest to me in the meeting was appointed. Other times, someone actually volunteered. I obviously had no clue what I was doing in terms of leadership development, but I just knew I had to transition ministry responsibility to Filipinos as soon as possible. For our first two years in the Philippines, anytime we were asked how long we intended to stay, our answer was, "About two more months." Two months after that, when we were asked the same question, we would answer, "About two more months."

In the early days, empowering young people for ministry and leadership was often driven by emergency rather than strategy. In time, our team developed a strategy that has helped us do a much better job of identifying potential leaders. The principle of identification has evolved to include five essentials we're looking for in a potential leader.

In the identification phase of our leadership-development strategy, we are trying to identify people who exhibit F.A.I.T.H. When I say we are looking for F.A.I.T.H., I mean that we're looking for potential leaders who are Faithful, Available, Involved, Teachable, and Hungry. Let's take a look.

1. **Faithful.** Our starting point for a potential leader is a person who is faithful. For me, "faithful" means, first and foremost, *faithful to God*. While I haven't taken a single seminary class on faithfulness, Jesus seemed to think faithfulness was pretty important for potential leaders and included it in His "seminary" training of the twelve. He

said that the person "who is faithful in a very little is also faithful in much, and one who is dishonest in a very little is also dishonest in much" (Luke 16:10). He then asked two rhetorical questions, "If then you have not been faithful in the unrighteous wealth, who will entrust to you the true riches? And if you have not been faithful in that which is another's, who will give you that which is your own?" (Luke 16:11–12).

In this passage, Jesus mentioned three areas of faithfulness that can cause promotion or stagnation for potential leaders. First, Jesus expects potential leaders to be faithful in "very little" things. Everyone gets serious when a big task is given, but Jesus expects our best even in the "very little" things. Second, Jesus wants His potential leaders to be faithful in "unrighteous wealth" before they can expect "true riches" to be entrusted to them. How potential leaders handle money says a lot about whether or not they are ready for the next level of leadership. And finally, Jesus expects potential leaders to be faithful with "that which is another's" before He is willing to give them something of their own. When we find someone who is faithful with little things, money, and things that are not their own, we've identified a potential leader.

2. Available. When the opportunity arose for Jun and Ferdie to conduct the Rock Seminar, they were chosen because they were available. They weren't trained, they weren't experts, they weren't very good at it, but they were available. Some people are extremely faithful, but never rise to the next level of leadership because they're also extremely busy. Many are way too busy to be available for God. Modern, driven Christians seem to think that busyness is the tenth fruit of the Spirit. It doesn't matter how much potential a person has, if that person is too busy to be used by God, then I cannot help him maximize his leadership potential. If you want to find potential leaders, look for people who are willing to make themselves available to God, to His church, and to you. Look for people with a "Here I am! Send me!" mentality (Isaiah 6:8).

3. Involved. When I needed someone to take my place at that Rock Seminar, I didn't ask a pastor from a more established church if I could borrow or hire a staff member. I also didn't pick someone from our little church who was sitting around doing nothing. Lazy people who do nothing might be available, but that isn't enough. I'm only interested in working with people who are available and involved at some level in what we're already doing. When I'm looking to invest more leadership responsibility, I look for people who are already involved in the local church and its mission. I'm not interested in people who church-hop, who are half-committed to their local church, and who do nothing while waiting for a personal invitation to minister or lead. They might be available, but they're not involved. When I find someone who has been involved in the local church and faithful in the little parts of the mission, then I'm willing to entrust them with more and more and more, and they rarely let me down. So, if you want to identify your next leaders, don't look for them outside of your church or campus ministry. Look for people who are already involved.

4. Teachable. When I say I look for people who are teachable, I mean people who are humble and willing to learn, grow, and receive correction. People who aren't willing to learn, grow, and receive correction apparently already know more than their leaders, and therefore, have already maximized their leadership potential. I don't have time for those people, and neither do you. People who think they already know more than their leaders need to move on and start something they can lead, somewhere else. The best way to see if a potential leader is teachable is to correct them. I suggest looking for an opportunity to bring kind and gracious correction as soon as possible, so you don't waste valuable time developing a potential leader who turns out to be unteachable. Ultimately, God's Word brings correction and training to a potential leader. "All Scripture is breathed out by God and profitable for teaching, for reproof, for correction, and for training in righteousness . . ." (2 Timothy 3:16). After letting God's Word bring correction, see if the person loves or hates it. If he loves correction, then you've identified a potential leader who is worthy of your time. If he hates correction, then you might want to look for someone else to develop because "whoever hates correction is stupid" (Proverbs 12:1, NIV). No one has time to invest in stupid leaders.

5. **Hungry.** When I look for hungry people, I'm looking for people who want to grow. Being teachable and being hungry are closely related because they're both rooted in humility. Humble people are teachable and willing to embrace correction. Humble people are hungry to grow and learn. When I find someone who's hungry for more knowledge, training, and responsibility, I know I've found a potential leader. I'm happy to do what I can to help him grow to the next level. But the main hunger I look for is a hunger for God's Word. Job said: "I have treasured the words of his mouth more than my portion of food" (Job 23:12). Notice how Jeremiah described his hunger for God's Word: "Your words were found, and I ate them, and your words became to me a joy and the delight of my heart, for I am called by

your name, O Lord, God of hosts" (Jeremiah 15:16). When you identify someone with an insatiable hunger for God's Word, you've identified a potential leader.

It doesn't matter how young, inexperienced, uneducated, unimpressive, or poor people may be, when they are faithful to God, available to serve, involved in church, teachable in spirit, and hungry for God's Word, you know you've identified potential leaders. At that point, you know you can invest your time and energy into helping them become the leaders God called them to be. When you find F.A.I.T.H., you have identified potential leaders.

IDENTIFYING POTENTIAL

As soon as we find men and women with F.A.I.T.H., we need to help them identify their calling, strengths, and opportunities.

Legendary American football coach Vince Lombardi often talked to his players about leadership. One of his most famous sayings was, "Leaders are made, they are not born." Being a natural-born follower, I completely agree with Coach Lombardi's maxim. However, I would suggest that before leaders are made, they must first be identified as potential leaders by other leaders.

It's almost always true that an established leader sees the potential in a future leader before the rest of the world sees it. Identifying potential may seem like an obvious principle in leadership development, but it's easy to overlook because potential is rather elusive and invisible. Undeveloped and underdeveloped potential is almost impossible for the untrained eye to detect. But for those who are intentionally, prayerfully, and desperately searching for future leaders,

God will give small hints of the potential that's buried under multiple layers of insecurity, pride, fear, and ambition.

I love it when people around me are puzzled as to why I would equip and empower certain people who seemingly have zero leadership abilities. I love it even more when those same doubters have to admit that these unlikely leaders often end up becoming great leaders.

The Bible has countless examples of unlikely leaders who became great leaders as soon as someone identified a small hint of leadership potential, then invested in them and empowered them to lead.

Think about David before he became king of Israel. When Samuel came to look at Jesse's sons in order to anoint a new king, David (who was out tending sheep) wasn't even invited to the meeting. His father and brothers apparently didn't think David had much leadership potential. Samuel was impressed with several of Jesse's sons, but God said to Samuel:

> . . . Do not look on his appearance or on the height of his stature, because I have rejected him. For the Lord sees not as man sees: man looks on the outward appearance, but the Lord looks on the heart. (1 Samuel 16:7)

It is interesting that even though Samuel needed a little help from God to identify David's leadership potential, God still chose to use a man to identify and anoint David as the next king. And while there are exceptions to the rule, this story of an established leader (Samuel) identifying a potential leader (David) is typical of how leadership development usually works, both in the Bible and in my personal experience.

Whether it's Samuel identifying David, Moses identifying Joshua (Numbers 27), Jesus identifying Peter (Matthew 16), Barnabas identifying Paul (Acts 9), or Paul identifying Timothy (Acts 16), the Bible is full of examples of established leaders identifying future leaders—sometimes with the explicit prompting of the Holy Spirit (Moses and Joshua), other times with an implicit leading (Paul and Timothy). In either case, the essential first step to training and empowering a future Joshua or a future Timothy is to identify them. However, the principle of identification is not just about an established leader identifying a potential leader. It's also about the established leader helping potential leaders identify their calling, gifting, and open doors.

IDENTIFYING CALLING

Calling is a difficult thing to discern for anyone, but the call to vocational ministry and church leadership is particularly difficult. People often confuse the call to make disciples (which is for everyone) with the call to vocational ministry (which is for some).

As a pastor, I've had countless conversations with young leaders who were either considering ministry or on the verge of leaving ministry. I've advised young leaders in different directions depending on their circumstances, gifts, and perceived calling. One of the more memorable of those calling conversations happened in a T.G.I. Friday's restaurant in Manila in 1996.

Deborah and I were having lunch with our friends, Ariel and Shirley. Ariel was in his late twenties and had gotten saved ten years earlier as a sophomore at De La Salle

University during a Rock Seminar. Soon after graduation, we hired him as our church accountant.

As I watched Ariel grow as a leader, I felt that maybe he was called to pastoral ministry. He seemed to have good pastoral instincts and potential as a relational leader. When I asked him if he would consider shifting roles from accountant to pastor, he was reluctant; but he eventually agreed to a pastoral role with one condition—that he would not have to preach. With that negotiation accepted, Ariel the accountant became Pastor Ariel, and he and Shirley started working with the young couples in our church.

It didn't take long for everyone to realize that this was a perfect fit for Ariel and Shirley. Under their leadership, our young family ministry took off. And before Ariel's first year as a pastor was finished, I even managed to get him to preach a Sunday sermon during the summer while I was in North America raising mission support.

However, toward the end of his first year as a pastor, Ariel had a few business opportunities that seemed rather lucrative at the time. Soon, he began to doubt whether he was called to vocational ministry and seriously considered leaving the ministry to pursue the business opportunity. And while I have sometimes counseled people to leave the ministry for other careers, I was convinced that Ariel was called to ministry.

As Deborah and I sat in the restaurant with Ariel and Shirley, I listened to his thoughts on leaving the ministry and asked him questions about the business opportunity he was considering. At the end of our conversation, I looked at Ariel and told him that the decision was his, but that I strongly felt that he was called to preach the gospel (which was kind of funny for a pastor who didn't want to preach).

After wrestling with God in prayer, Ariel and Shirley decided to stay in the ministry.

They worked on my staff at Victory Valle Verde for five years, then we assigned Ariel and Shirley to our new Quezon City congregation. After serving in Quezon City for a year, a spot opened up for a senior pastor position in our Alabang congregation. I asked Ariel if he would consider being the interim senior pastor in Alabang, and he (reluctantly again) said yes. By this time, he had voluntarily broken his vow of silence and had become an effective preacher.

Fifteen years later, Ariel is still preaching and leading Victory Alabang—a congregation that has grown from around 600 to over 10,000 under his leadership, including over 800 Victory group leaders.

In a recent discussion with Ariel, I asked him what he thinks would have happened had he gone into business instead of ministry in 1996. He answered: "I'm not sure. I'd probably be miserable. I'm so glad I decided to stay in the ministry, and I'm grateful I was given the opportunity to serve Victory Alabang."

Calling to vocational ministry isn't an easy thing to discern. However, I believe that God will guide gifted and humble men and women into their ministry calling. He can use whatever means He wants, but in my experience, He usually uses established leaders to help emerging leaders identify and understand their calling.

IDENTIFYING SPIRITUAL GIFTS

God not only calls leaders, He also graciously provides the spiritual gifts necessary for success. Established leaders must help potential leaders identify their spiritual gifts.

Why? Because even though gifts and talents are God-given, they're often undiscovered and undeveloped. Furthermore, many of us are so insecure in who God has made us to be, we need someone else to help us recognize the gifts and talents that He has put inside of us.

A few months before Jun and Ferdie led their first Rock Seminar, I had a lunch meeting with Jun, who was a fresh graduate. In the meeting, I asked him about his post-graduation plans. He told me about a job opportunity to work on a ship. I then asked him to write down some of his dreams. His biggest dream was to become a political leader in his province.

I then asked him if he would consider praying about serving in the ministry. He was surprised by my suggestion, but he agreed to consider it and pray about it. While I believe that Christians should engage in politics, after discipling Jun for eighteen months, I had observed leadership and ministry gifts that I knew could be further developed if he was willing to make himself available. I feared that if Jun took the job on that ship, his leadership potential would sail with him to the seven seas and remain undeveloped.

I had identified Jun as a gifted leader with a great future in our church, but he didn't yet fully see what I saw. When I asked him to lead the Rock Seminar that day, the results helped convince him of the magnitude of his leadership potential. It also opened his eyes to his evangelistic preaching gift.

Over twenty-five years after his first Rock Seminar, Jun sees that moment as a major turning point in his leadership development. He says it was the first time he fully recognized his evangelistic gifting and his ability to effectively exegete a culture in order to communicate the gospel. After several years of leading our Rock Seminar evangelistic outreaches in the 1980s, today, there's not one university or high school in Manila's University Belt where Jun hasn't presented a Rock Seminar and led a student to Christ.

After serving as a campus missionary, a church planter, and a mission director, Jun eventually earned a doctorate in missiology. Today, he serves as the director of Every Nation's Asia Regional Leadership Team. He also leads the Every Nation School of World Missions, which trains and sends cross-cultural missionaries all over Asia and the world. I am honored and humbled that God allowed me to be part of helping Jun discover his evangelistic, apostolic, and leadership gifts.

God put spiritual gifts in Jun. I didn't put them there. But He used people, including me, to help Jun discover and develop those gifts. More often than not, that's how it works. There's a supernatural part, and there's a human part.

IDENTIFYING OPPORTUNITIES AND OPEN DOORS

After identifying divine calling and spiritual gifts in a person, the next step is to help potential leaders discern open doors and leadership opportunities.

"'Behold, I have set before you an open door, which no one is able to shut'" (Revelation 3:8). This verse teaches us that God creates doors. He opens doors. He puts doors before us. And He makes sure no one can shut His doors. But it's our responsibility to find the open doors and walk through them.

I suspect that there are countless open doors that no one ever discovers or walks through, and that's a sad thought.

I want to maximize every door that God opens for me and for the potential leaders around me.

Paul's comment to the Corinthians about his open door reveals one reason some open doors are ignored: ". . . a wide door for effective work has opened to me, and there are many adversaries" (1 Corinthians 16:9). Established leaders need to help new leaders identify their open doors. They also need to teach future leaders that life won't necessarily be easy just because God opens a door for them. The more open doors we have, the more adversaries we will have.

When I look back on my journey, I realize that some of the most significant turning points in my leadership development occurred simply because someone identified an open door for me, and I walked through it.

When I think about the power of recognizing and walking through open doors, I'm reminded of the leadership journey of my friend, Robert Hern, Jr., who I mentioned in chapter 2.

Robert got saved as a college student in the U-Belt in 1988. He quickly got involved in the life of the church and volunteered to help with a church plant in Angeles, a city a few hours north of Manila. As a college student, he would go to Angeles on the weekends with a team from Manila to lead worship services. One weekend, the worship leader from Manila wasn't able to go, so the pastor leading the outreach asked Robert to lead worship.

At the time, Robert was a new believer, an eighteen-year-old college student, and had never led worship before. He had never even volunteered on the worship team, but he agreed to lead worship that Sunday. Today, he still claims that he was pretty lousy, but the pastor who led the outreach saw something in him and asked him to lead worship not only during the weekend outreaches in Angeles, but also in the regular Sunday services at Victory U-Belt.

Robert led worship at Victory U-Belt for nearly a decade, becoming one of Victory's best worship leaders—often leading worship at conferences and joint services. He was definitely not one of the best singers, but over the years, he learned how to lead people into worship—a skill that has very little to do with the quality of one's voice.

After ten years of leading worship at U-Belt, Robert was able to develop as a leader through three different open doors. The first was in 1999 when he was part of a church-planting team in New Manila. The second was in 2001 when he became the head administrator at Victory Ortigas. The third open door was in 2005 when he came on my staff at Every Nation Philippines as the Director of Operations.

Robert excelled in each of these job opportunities and found himself learning new skills in each role. At every job, he was content to stay, but when the next door opened, his pastors always encouraged him to prayerfully consider where God's next step might take him. Looking back now, Robert realizes that, in each season, his leadership skills were being developed in unique ways.

In 2008, I asked Robert if he would be interested in serving as senior pastor of Victory Pioneer, our newest congregation in Metro Manila. Robert was hesitant to take on the responsibility of senior pastor, saying "no" several times. But after a couple of months of thinking and praying, Robert finally agreed to lead Victory Pioneer.

Robert, who had been a dynamic worship leader and an excellent administrator, simply didn't see himself as a senior pastor. However, he agreed to give it a try because our team believed in him. When Robert started leading

Victory Pioneer in 2008, the church had about 700 people involved. After six years, the congregation grew to over 8,000 in weekly attendance.

Robert and his family recently relocated to Southern California to plant Victory San Diego. Victory Pioneer continues to grow explosively, and Victory San Diego has gotten off to a great start. Just thirteen months after its first worship service, Robert and Victory San Diego are already starting Victory Pasadena.

God opened a door for me in the Philippines, and He used Rice Broocks to let me know the door was open. God opened multiple doors for ministry and leadership for Robert Hern, and He used our team to make Robert aware of the opportunities. Here's how it usually works: God opens doors, and He uses people to help us identify and walk through those doors. For those who choose to walk alone, God opens doors. But without the help of friends, the independent potential leader often doesn't even notice that the door exists.

When I think about the ministry trajectories of Jun, Ferdie, Ariel, and Robert, it's clear that God was actively involved in their leadership development. He gifted each of them uniquely. He called each of them specifically. He opened the right doors at the right time. However, at each stage, God used established leaders to help Jun, Ferdie, Ariel, and Robert identify and understand their call, their gifts, and their opportunities.

Left to ourselves, most of us simply will not see the enormity of our God-given leadership potential. Thankfully, God often provides experienced leaders to help us identify our leadership calling, spiritual gifts, and ministry opportunities.

If you're an established leader, you are responsible not only to lead, but also to help identify the next leader. That's how you rise to the challenge of multiplying leaders. Identifying a future leader by finding F.A.I.T.H. is the starting point. Next, we have to help potential leaders receive instruction from God's Word.

DISCUSSION QUESTIONS X

1. How would you introduce yourself?
2. Who helped you identify your calling? How did he or she help?
3. Who are you helping? How?
4. Which of the F.A.I.T.H. traits do you think is hardest to find in a potential leader? How can you help potential leaders grow in that area?

7

INSTRUCTION

The mediocre teacher tells. The good teacher explains. The superior teacher demonstrates. The great teacher inspires.

WILLIAM ARTHUR WARD, Writer

Learning is ever in the freshness of its youth, even for the old.

AESCHYLUS, Ancient Greek Tragedian

Give instruction to a wise man, and he will be still wiser; teach a righteous man, and he will increase in learning.

PROVERBS 9:9

When I was a new campus missionary, it didn't seem like anyone really aspired to have a teaching ministry. There was an unspoken but well-established ministry pecking order, and teachers were near the bottom of the pile. World-changing apostles were the top dogs, with bold, boisterous evangelists right behind them. Mystical, miracle-working prophets were seeded third, and calm, faithful pastors rounded out God's top four.

Teachers were a distant fifth, barely a notch above "lowly" administrators and regular church members.

Of course, big tithers and small celebrities weren't regular church members, so they could be elevated above everyone on the spiritual totem pole (except apostles). Apostles always occupied the top spot.

I'm not suggesting that any of this was healthy or right, but from my perspective, it seemed to be the way ministry worked.

With this as my context, you can imagine how thrilled I was when itinerant prophetic ministers visited our little student church in Mississippi and labeled me a teacher. I felt insulted and silently screamed, "Nooo, I do NOT want to be a teacher. Anything but a teacher!"

But, year after year, prophet after prophet continued to brand me with the dreaded teacher tag. Eventually, I figured that I had no option but to surrender to the call and take my position at the end of the leadership line with the teachers and administrators.

As I studied the Bible, I grew to understand and embrace the call to teach. When Victory Manila started growing, rather than surround myself with like-gifted team members, I intentionally filled our staff with non-teachers who were young evangelists, prophets, pastors, apostles, and administrators. My strategy was to make up for the ministry gifts that I lacked. Having a multi-gifted leadership team enabled me to maximize my teaching gift. With others doing what they were great at, I spent the bulk of my time writing foundational Bible study books, discipleship-training courses, small-group study guides, leadership-development material, and just about anything and everything a young growing church might need to equip and empower wave after wave of fledgling leaders.

Looking back now, it's difficult to understand why I didn't immediately accept and celebrate the call to be a teacher. Even if my ministry community didn't fully appreciate the importance of teaching, the Bible made it abundantly clear that instruction is not an afterthought, but is of central importance.

When Jesus sent out His original twelve disciples, He instructed them about where to go, what to avoid, who to minister to, and what to preach. He also included instructions about healing, miracles, demons, and financial matters. He even instructed them on what to pack for their journey, where to stay, and how to respond to rejection. Jesus certainly didn't see teaching and instruction as unimportant. (See Matthew 10:5–15.)

Just as Jesus taught and instructed His disciples, He expected them to teach and instruct future generations of disciples. His Great Commission stresses the importance of instruction: "Go therefore and make disciples of all nations, baptizing them in the name of the Father and of the Son and of the Holy Spirit, teaching them to observe all that I have commanded you" (Matthew 28:19–20). Notice that the type of instruction Jesus expects is more than simply transferring information. We are supposed to teach people to observe, obey, and act on His commands.

INTELLECTUAL TRAINING

Jesus identified His twelve, then He gave them instructions. Likewise, once we identify our potential leaders, we need to provide the instruction they will need to become the leaders God has called them to be. Instruction is not something that we start and finish, and then we proceed to the next principle of the leadership-development strategy. For the serious leader, instruction is a lifelong endeavor. A leader might finish an academic degree, but learning is never finished.

In the last chapter, I said you should look for leaders who are faithful, available, involved, teachable, and hungry. Those last two words, teachable and hungry, indicate a person who is ready to make learning a lifestyle.

We should never underestimate the power of timely instruction. Every leader can point to moments of instruction that were life-altering.

I still remember the day Ferdie Cabiling and I walked into our first class at Asian Theological Seminary (ATS) in Quezon City, just north of Manila. It was in the early 1990s. Victory Manila was about ten years old. With the growth of Victory, we were extremely busy, but we were also eager to learn, so we enrolled in seminary. We were paying a high price to learn. Not a monetary price, but a stress price. That stress had to do with Manila's infamous traffic.

Manila traffic cannot be described with words. It's impossible to explain it to people who have not experienced it, but let me try anyway. If Dante were to add another level to hell, it would be Manila's rush hour traffic, especially during rainy season. I've never understood why, but during Manila's typhoon season, vehicles multiply and roads shrink. But, as miserable as our commute to ATS was, nothing could keep Ferdie and I away.

I don't remember what degree track I was on, but Ferdie and I walked into our first class ready to listen and learn. My strategy was to take a wide range of classes in order to find the best professors and then take as many of their classes as possible. Hopefully, those classes would add up to some kind of degree, but if not, no problem. My goal was to learn as much as I could, not necessarily to get a degree.

When I refer to *instruction* in this chapter and the remainder of this book, I'm referring to the transfer of useful information to a potential leader—information that will shape their character, inform their decision-making, and give them the necessary information to succeed in their leadership context. As I mentioned before, instruction as a principle of leadership development is not only about the transfer of knowledge; it's about teaching people how to learn and how to think. In other words, instruction is about training the mind of the leader. No athlete expects to compete at the Olympic level without consistent and disciplined physical training. And no leader should expect to change the world without consistent and disciplined intellectual training.

Nowhere is the passion for learning more explicit than in the book of Proverbs. Here's how it opens:

> The proverbs of Solomon son of David, king of Israel: for attaining wisdom and discipline; for understanding words of insight; for acquiring a disciplined and prudent life, doing what is right and just and fair; for giving prudence to the simple, knowledge and discretion to the young—let the wise listen and add to their learning, and let the discerning get guidance—for understanding proverbs and parables, the sayings and riddles of the wise. The fear of the Lord is the beginning of knowledge, but fools despise wisdom and discipline. Listen, my son, to your father's instruction and do not forsake your mother's teaching. (Proverbs 1:1–8, NIV)

Whenever I read Proverbs, I'm continually reminded that, as a leader, I should always be seeking instruction ("let the wise and add to their learning . . ."). I'm also reminded that as a leader, I should be instructing emerging leaders in wisdom—as Solomon does in the book of Proverbs ("Listen, my son, to your father's instruction . . .").

In some church circles, intellectual instruction is frowned upon as though it is anti-spiritual. It's almost as though many people would rather skip this principle of leadership development altogether. We like the discovery of *identification*—helping people identify their gifting, calling, and open doors. We like the adventure of *impartation*—building close relationships that lead to personal growth. And we like the excitement of *internship*—learning new skills through on-the-job training with experienced leaders.

But we don't like the mental labor of *instruction*—committing ourselves to disciplined study, opening ourselves to new ideas, and applying our minds to questions that don't have easy answers and immediate applications.

"But when am I going to use this information?" This is often the complaint about instruction, whether in a church context or a university general education class. And while I'm a practitioner at heart and have little patience for thinking that's disconnected from doing, I know that it's important for future leaders to embrace instruction as a long-term investment. Hopefully, the content learned will be applicable to your leadership context someday, but even if not, the discipline of applying your mind to learning will make you a better leader today and for the rest of your life.

Sometimes, the underlying issue with young leaders who are resistant to instruction is pride. They simply don't think there's much more for them to learn—at least from those leading them. This is a serious problem for both the established leader and the potential leader. If you're an established leader with young leaders who don't want to learn, then perhaps you've identified the wrong people to lead. And if you're an emerging leader who thinks that you have little to learn from your leader, then you might be a fool—for "fools despise wisdom and instruction," according to Solomon (Proverbs 1:7).

JESUS VALUED INSTRUCTION; DO YOU?

When we look at the Gospels, we usually talk about what Jesus taught or what He did. But we often forget that Matthew, Mark, Luke, and John primarily cover the last three years of Jesus' life. Besides the circumstances surrounding His birth, what happened during the first thirty years of His life is largely unknown. However, one of the only stories in the Gospels about Jesus' life before beginning ministry is one in which He is seeking instruction. It's a rather odd story, but here's my quick summary of Luke 2:43–52.

Jesus traveled to Jerusalem with His family to attend a Jewish religious feast. "And when the feast was ended, as they were returning, the boy Jesus stayed behind in Jerusalem. His parents did not know it, but supposing him to be in the group they went a day's journey, but then they began to search for him among their relatives and acquaintances . . ." When Joseph and Mary realized Jesus wasn't with the group, they returned to Jerusalem to find him.

"After three days they found him *in the temple, sitting among the teachers, listening to them and asking them questions.* And all who heard him were amazed at his understanding and his answers."

The story ends with a statement that is true of all people, especially potential leaders, who are teachable and hungry for instruction: "And Jesus increased in wisdom and in stature and in favor with God and man."

I've always found this story interesting and a bit puzzling. Here we have young Jesus—God incarnate—staying behind in Jerusalem to learn from the teachers of the law. But what did He have to learn? Didn't He already know everything? What's more—why did He choose to learn from the teachers of the law in the temple? They were the very same people who would one day speak out against His ministry and plot to kill Him. Why would He attempt to learn from them?

To be honest, I don't know. This story brings up all sorts of theological questions about Jesus' humanity and divinity, and how both operated in the same person at the same time—similar questions that are brought up by the story of His baptism.

However, one thing I do know from this story is that Jesus sought and valued instruction. He was a learner, "sitting among the teachers, listening to them and asking them questions." He didn't think that instruction was beneath Him. Rather, He sat humbly at the feet of established leaders. He didn't critique them for upholding the letter of law and misunderstanding the spirit of law (at least not yet), but He sat at their feet because they were experts in the law.

Jesus sought and valued instruction. Do you?

We often forget about this story because the Gospels cover such a short snapshot of His life, but I imagine this wasn't the only time Jesus sat at the feet of the teachers of the law in the temple or at the local synagogue.

A WORTHWHILE INVESTMENT

In Jesus' day, instruction happened primarily in the temple and in the synagogue. Today, instruction happens in a variety of places, formats, and contexts. The church has multiple forms of instruction and spiritual education—seminaries, Bible colleges, church-based training schools, podcasts, and other forms of online education. Though all are valid, some are more useful than others depending on one's educational needs and ministry calling. It's important for church leaders to discover the best learning opportunities for themselves and their potential leaders given their individual ministry calling.

For example, if a young leader felt called to be a cross-cultural missionary in Mongolia, it probably wouldn't be very helpful to pursue a degree in Systematic Theology from a traditional Western seminary. On the other hand, if a young leader wanted to engage the highly intellectual culture of a city like Boston or Berlin, it would probably be helpful to pursue an education beyond what most churches include in their in-house Bible schools.

The question is not "Seminary or no seminary?" The question is: What type of instruction is most useful, given the calling and gifting of each individual?

At Victory, we have used different types of instruction in our obsessive attempt to train leaders. I mentioned one of those methods in a previous chapter, the "Leadership Lab," which was a series of summer intensives designed to equip and empower university students to do small-group discipleship when they returned to campus.

Over the years, we also made consistent efforts to bring in outside speakers to further develop our upcoming leaders. Later, I was surprised to learn how many of our leaders cited intensive leadership seminars taught by guest speakers as vital in their leadership development. Some of the perennial favorites included Kevin Conner, a brilliant Bible teacher from Australia; Jim Laffoon, a prophet from the United States; Timothy Loh, a pastor and teacher from Malaysia; Dr. Greg Mitchell, a pastor from Canada; Bruce Fidler, a Bible teacher from Nashville; Paul Barker, a teacher and trainer from Nashville, and many others. While it can be expensive to fly in teachers from around the world, providing sound instruction for your leaders is a worthwhile investment.

As our church grew larger and larger, Victory started having opportunities to host meetings for famous celebrity preachers. Their offices would inform us that they were in the area and offer their services. We declined almost every time. It didn't matter how famous a person might be, how many bestsellers he wrote, or how many nations his television ministry had reached. Unless I personally knew him to have stellar integrity, sound doctrine, and respect for our mission and values, I would graciously decline the opportunity to have him minister to our leaders. Some of my ministry friends were surprised that I wasn't interested in hosting certain world-famous preachers. My reason for passing up the opportunities made perfect sense to me. I stayed in Manila to equip and empower multiple generations of Filipino leaders, not to host international preachers who might inadvertently confuse our people with a different vision or ministry style. Also, I had no interest in hosting famous preachers who would attract Christians from other churches to Victory.

THE TOP FOUR SOURCES OF INSTRUCTION

We can find instruction and education in so many places. But here are my top four sources of instruction for leadership development.

1. Classroom instruction. My life was forever changed by instruction from two Asian Theological Seminary professors, Dr. Nomer Bernardino and Dr. Larry Caldwell. Nomer was an Old Testament scholar who had several master's degrees, a post-graduate certificate in Middle East Studies from the Institute of Holy Land Studies in Jerusalem, and a Doctor of Ministry degree from Regent University. Besides teaching Genesis and a Survey of the Old Testament, Nomer also taught Hermeneutics (Bible interpretation) and Homiletics (preaching). Nomer was a powerful preacher and an excellent teacher. I took every class he taught. I only wish he had taught more subjects.

Nomer's class on the book of Genesis made a tremendous impact on my understanding of the Bible and my preaching. My understanding of covenant, atonement, multi-generational leadership, sacrifice, obedience, worship, generosity, and faith were all shaped by Nomer's Genesis lectures.

Two of Larry Caldwell's classes made an impact on my life and ministry as much as Nomer's Genesis class. The first was a missiological study of the book of Acts. The second was called Ethno-Hermeneutics (Bible interpretation done in multi-generational, multi-cultural, and cross-cultural contexts). Larry's lectures were always instructive, but his class activities, rigorous discussions, and thought-provoking homework assignments made his classes a life-changing learning experience. He created a learning environment that was creative, participatory, and transformational. Whether he was teaching the book of Acts, Ethno-Hermeneutics, or missiology, Larry's lectures presented well-known passages in new ways that challenged me to rethink my assumptions.

I am forever grateful to Nomer and Larry for presenting instruction that changed my life. And I'm more convinced than ever that if we want to develop the next level of leaders in our churches and campus ministries, we will need to provide quality instruction.

For many years, as mentioned in chapter 5, our primary means for leadership instruction at Victory Manila was our in-house Bible school—Every Nation Leadership Institute (ENLI). The first-year module covered Old and New Testament survey, church history, and basic ministry skills. The second year included leadership, discipleship, and theology courses. For several years, ENLI did a joint venture with ATS that enabled our students to get seminary credit for their ENLI classes. Although that collaboration was successful on many levels, we eventually decided that the extra cost to our students for seminary accreditation just wasn't worth it. We continued the same level of instruction, but at a lower cost and without official seminary credit.

We are constantly evaluating and upgrading our instruction. What we do today is not what we did ten years ago. And what we will do next year is not what we will do in twenty years. As campus ministries, local churches, and global movements grow and expand, their method of instruction must also grow and expand. Hopefully, we're getting better and better with each change. As I write this chapter, we're putting the finishing touches on a new global leadership-development curriculum called Leadership 215, which is designed to upgrade the theological foundations of current and upcoming Every Nation pastors all over the world. We are also in the preliminary stages of developing an accredited theological seminary.

2. Sunday sermons. Right now, I'm fifty-six years old. That means I first heard, understood, and responded to the gospel forty years ago as a sixteen-year-old high school student. That happened at First Presbyterian Church's youth group in Jackson, Mississippi. I immediately got involved in the First Pres youth group, but only attended their Sunday worship services once. In my sixteen-year-old expert opinion, the Sunday dress code was restrictive, the music was lame, and the sermon was boring. Except for the dress code, I would probably love their services today. Anyway, a few weeks after surrendering my life to Jesus, I visited New Covenant Church with my brother. New Covenant was an upstart independent Charismatic church with no dress code, contemporary music, and in-depth exegetical sermons.

Believe it or not, I still remember some of those New Covenant sermons forty years later. I was particularly influenced by an eighteen-month-long, verse-by-verse Sunday night sermon series on the book of Romans. I hated that I missed the final five months of the Romans series when I moved away to attend Mississippi State University. Unfortunately, in those days, we didn't have podcasts.

I'm thankful that, as a new believer, I found a church that was serious about teaching the Bible, rather than giving weekly motivational talks or success-in-life lectures. Those sermons shaped my life.

If you're a pastor, don't underestimate the transformational power of Christ-centered, Spirit-empowered sermons and well-planned, exegetical sermon series.

Paul certainly understood the power of preaching. He told the Corinthians:

> For Christ did not send me to baptize but to preach the gospel, and not with words of eloquent wisdom, lest the cross of Christ be emptied of its power. For the word of the cross is folly to those who are perishing, but to us who are being saved it is the power of God. (1 Corinthians 1:17–18)

3. **Personal study.** The best classroom instruction and the most meaningful Sunday sermons inspire us to personal study. And that is where real life change happens. Many times, after listening to a Nomer Bernardino Genesis lecture or a Larry Caldwell Ethno-Hermeneutics class discussion, I couldn't wait to get home to do more personal study. I wanted to be like those famous "more noble" Berean believers who "received the word with all eagerness, *examining the Scriptures daily* to see if these things were so" (Acts 17:11).

I know it doesn't always happen, but one of my goals as a teacher is to present lectures and to create classroom environments that provoke my students to personal study. My prayer is for classrooms to be filled with Bereans who receive "the word with all eagerness, examining the Scriptures daily."

Almost twenty years ago, in the spirit of that eighteen-month New Covenant Church sermon series on the book of Romans, I decided to teach through the book of Mark. At the time, Victory had two Manila locations—U-Belt and Makati. I had just handed off the U-Belt congregation to my friend, Luther Mancao, so I was only responsible for the two services at Makati Sports Club. My book of Mark

Sunday sermon series lasted two years. I hope it helped the congregation. I know it helped me.

Because I publicly committed to teach the whole book of Mark, I was forced to study passages that I usually skimmed over. Those two years in Mark were life-changing for me. I couldn't wait to dig deep into Mark each week, and my personal study of the Bible went to a new level.

A few years later, our leadership team made a decision that had an even greater impact on my personal study of God's Word. We decided that all our Victory Manila locations would synchronize their Sunday sermon series. This forced us to plan sermons months in advance and to write our sermons together in teams. Studying a topic or text with a team of serious Bible teachers forced my personal study to go even deeper.

Last week, Deborah and I were in Hawaii speaking at the International Apostolic Leadership Conference for my mentor and old friend, Emanuele Cannistraci. As always Deborah grabbed our favorite seats on the back row, where we got to meet another back-row leader, Pastor Charles Green. I had heard the legend of Charles for many years, but this was our first face-to-face meeting. As soon as I realized that he had been an avid biker most of his life, we instantly hit if off (even though he rides an American Harley and I ride a German 1200GS).

Over the three days of the conference, I noticed that Pastor Green not only had an engaging sense of humor, but he also constantly quoted Scripture. I don't mean his speech was sprinkled with paraphrased Bible verses. I mean he quoted huge chunks of the Bible, word for word, straight from the King James Version.

During one conversation, as Pastor Green narrated the history of his influential New Orleans church, I noticed that he quoted Romans 10:2–13 effortlessly. He was trying to explain to me why he named the church Word of Faith, so as he quoted eleven verses in Romans 10, he emphasized verse 8, "But what saith it? The word is nigh thee, even in thy mouth, and in thy heart: that is, the *word of faith*, which we preach . . ." He then gave the most biblically balanced and theologically sound explanation of "word of faith" that I have ever heard. I wish I had recorded it on my phone.

During his teaching session on the second day, without notes, Pastor Green rattled off Hebrews 1:1–9, with special emphasis on the supremacy of Christ. Again, his message (still without any notes) was biblical, inspirational, and doctrinally sound.

This man, who was flawlessly quoting Bible verse after Bible verse, was one month away from his ninetieth birthday. I'm only fifty-six, and I can't remember where I parked my car.

I asked Pastor Green if he used a systematic and disciplined regimen to memorize Scripture, or if certain verses just stuck in his mind because he studied, preached, and prayed those particular verses so much.

He smiled and said that he never intentionally memorizes Bible passages, but because of personal Bible study, he simply cannot forget many verses.

I'm certainly not suggesting that you shouldn't intentionally memorize God's Word. I'm saying that if you study diligently and consistently, you won't be able to forget what you plant deep in your heart.

In order to upgrade your personal study of God's Word, I suggest you invest in a good study Bible. I use the ESV Study Bible. I also recommend Logos Bible Software, a virtual library you can carry with you everywhere you go, inside your computer or tablet.

A disciplined and strategic commitment to personal Bible study is essential if you want to "Do your best to present yourself to God as one approved, a worker who has no need to be ashamed, rightly handling the word of truth" (2 Timothy 2:15).

4. Good books. Our discussion about personal study above focused on studying the Bible. Another aspect of personal study involves reading good books. Some of my greatest growth as a leader has come from applying the wisdom and instruction of people who haven't taught a class for hundreds of years. I've read many books over the years that have profoundly influenced the way I lead. Some were recommended and others I just stumbled upon, but I can't imagine where I would be as a leader had I not read certain books along the way.

Here are ten books that have had the greatest impact on my life and ministry. I've read most of these multiple times.

- *The Pursuit of God* **by A. W. Tozer.** When I read this as a new believer, it ignited a lifelong desire to pursue and please God wholeheartedly. It reignites that same desire every time I reread a chapter.

- *The Holiness of God* **by R. C. Sproul.** My eyes were opened the first time I read this book. My heart was opened the second time. My heart was pierced the third time. My heart was healed the fourth time. Every time I read this book, I go deeper with God.

- *Knowing God* **by J. I. Packer.** This classic helped me know God and made me want to know Him better. This is another book I have read over and over and over. Today, it's held together by duct tape.

- *A History of Christianity: Beginnings to 1500 (Volume 1)* by Kenneth Scott Latourette. Everything Latourette wrote about history is worth reading, but his early church history is the best. His experience as a missionary to China and later as a professor of Ecclesiastical History at Yale University gave him a unique perspective on the expansion of the church. The combination of missional passion and scholarly detail make these 700 pages read like an adventure novel.

- *The Making of a Leader* by Frank Damazio. More than any book that isn't the Bible, this book influenced how I think about leadership, how I lead, and how I equip and empower leaders.

- *Spiritual Leadership* by J. Oswald Sanders. Another book from my shelf that's held together by duct tape, I have worn out several copies of this leadership classic. It doesn't matter how many times I read it, I always learn something new.

- *No Wonder They Call Him the Savior* by Max Lucado. I've lost count of how many times I've read this one. It taught me that complicated, difficult-to-understand theological concepts can and should be communicated with a clarity and simplicity that even a child can comprehend.

- *The Church in the New Testament* by Kevin J. Conner. There isn't a book in my office more highlighted and underlined than this one. It was my constant companion during the first ten years of Victory Manila.

- *C. T. Studd* by Norman Grubb. This was the first missionary biography I read as a new believer. The C. T. Studd story planted seeds of sacrifice and service deep in my soul as a teenager. I'm not sure I would have stayed in Manila had I not read this foundational book about absolute surrender to the Lordship of Christ for the sake of cross-cultural missions.

- *Lectures to My Students* by **Charles Spurgeon.** What would it be like to take a homiletics class taught by the "Prince of Preachers" himself? Read his book and find out. While I don't even almost preach like Spurgeon, his book sure provoked me to preach better.

Today, in the age of the Internet, we have greater access to free quality instruction than ever before. Podcasts, blogs, e-books, iTunes U, online reference material—you can learn so much without ever leaving the coffee shop. Since so much material is available, it's more important than ever for veteran leaders to be proactive in recommending good books and other resources to future leaders.

BACK TO SCHOOL AT FIFTY-SIX

The principle of instruction is vitally important because leaders on all levels make decisions—decisions that affect more people than just themselves. It's essential for established leaders to teach new leaders how to learn, how to think, and how to make wise decisions.

In my years of ministry, I've met far too many young and old leaders with good hearts but empty heads. These leaders frequently make bad leadership decisions that inadvertently hurt not only themselves, but also those following them. And when I refer to empty-headed leaders, I'm not talking about a lack of formal education. Many leaders with impressive academic degrees make some of the dumbest decisions imaginable, and some of the wisest and most thoughtful leaders don't have college degrees. Some haven't even finished high school.

What matters in the principle of *instruction* in leadership development isn't necessarily formal education, but a passionate desire to learn. Please don't misunderstand me. I am not anti-education. In fact, just this morning, I received the following e-mail.

> Congratulations! You are admitted to the Doctor of Ministry Program at Asbury Theological Seminary. Officially, your acceptance to "Preaching and Leading" signifies you have taken an admirable step toward a higher education degree that connects directly with your ministry context. We are excited to partner with you in this endeavor.

I am fifty-six years old, and I "have taken an admirable step toward a higher education degree" because I want to do my best to present myself to God "as one approved, a worker who has no need to be ashamed, rightly handling the word of truth" (2 Timothy 2:15).

Like my previous seminary experiences at Reformed Theological Seminary and Asian Theological Seminary, my next three years at Asbury are primarily about learning, not collecting initials after my name.

By the grace of God, I hope I never lose the desire to learn.

INSTRUCTIONS FOR THE INSTRUCTORS

If you have the responsibility of being the person giving instruction, here are five simple steps to help you become a better teacher.

1. Prepare the heart. The starting point is always the heart. In order to be the best teachers we can possibly be, we must diligently guard our hearts (Proverbs 4:23). Because even good hearts tend to wander, harden, and break, consistent Scripture reading is vital to refocus wandering hearts, soften hard hearts, and heal broken hearts.

Ultimately, it is Scripture that prepares the heart to teach. In *Eat This Book*, scholar Eugene Peterson likens a pastor reading and studying the Bible to a dog working a bone. The dog gnaws the bone, then buries it. The next day the dog digs up the bone, gnaws it, and buries it again. This process repeats itself for weeks. When a pastor consistently studies the Scriptures like a dog with a bone, healthy spiritual formation and heart preparation happens.

Like most teachers, Saint Augustine also wrestled with heart issues. He wondered if the very idea of fallen humans trying to understand the meaning of Scripture might be a prideful act of presumption. He wisely concluded that it would be presumptuous, if he were trusting in his own intellect. But since any hope of understanding God's Word demands complete reliance on Him, then there is no room for human pride.

While the heart of the teacher is prepared primarily through Scripture, it is also prepared and formed through community. Augustine taught that the prerequisite to good teaching and preaching was not only to love God, but also to love those we hope to instruct. In order to properly teach people, we must properly love those people. We must work on our relationships as we work on our message. God uses relationships to prepare our hearts, like iron sharpening iron and one man sharpening another.

2. Exegete the text. Once our hearts are prepared, we can turn our attention to the message itself. Assuming our teaching is Bible-based, if we want to be effective teachers, then we must properly exegete the Bible text. Before we can exegete the text, we have to clearly determine the parameters of the text—where the text actually begins and ends. Lazy teachers and preachers simply extract a few words or a sentence out of context to make a point. This is common, but unacceptable.

Biblical teaching is more concerned with faithfully interpreting the Bible than displaying our Bible knowledge by quoting multiple verses that are loosely related to a particular topic. Compiling long lists of Bible verses is the easy way to address a topic. Faithful interpretation is not easy. It is often time-consuming, but Holy Scripture demands nothing short of the teacher's full and faithful engagement with the text.

3. Exegete the context. It is not enough to properly exegete the text, only to misapply or miscommunicate it because we are ignorant of our audience; thus, the need to exegete the context.

As mentioned earlier in this chapter, I was fortunate to have taken several cross-cultural mission and Ethno-Hermeneutics classes at Asian Theological Seminary that addressed the need to exegete culture, community, and context. Unfortunately, it seems that the cross-cultural emphasis at ATS is perhaps the exception rather than the

Instruction

rule. Most seminaries and Bible schools go to great lengths to train students to exegete the text, but often do little to train them to exegete the context, culture, and community.

Most people accept that if a person moves to the other side of the planet as a cross-cultural missionary, then the new context will need to be studied. But we often fail to realize that our local context also needs to be studied, unless the whole community is the same age, gender, ethnicity, nationality, religion, and political view. Since that perfectly homogenous community does not exist, every teacher needs to exegete the context and use language appropriate to that context in order to effectively communicate the message.

4. Preach from the heart. Once the teacher has prepared the heart, studied the text and the context, then it's time to actually communicate the message. The best communication comes from the heart, not just the head.

If the message being communicated is a Sunday sermon, then it is important to remind yourself that no one should go to church to hear a preacher's words; they are there to hear God's Word. So, if you are preaching, you better show up with a word from God.

It is not enough just to have a word from God or a teaching based on God's Word; it is also vital that we use words that make sense to our context and community. Jesus taught with words that were appropriate for both the educated and uneducated, men and women, the religious and irreligious, and Jews and Gentiles.

5. Model the message. If we have a heart for God, a word from God, and we use words that make sense in our context, there is still at least one remaining task for the teacher or preacher. That task is to be an example of what we teach.

In other words, we must not only mouth the message, we must model the message. We must be a living illustration of what we teach.

The Apostle James said that those who teach without being a doer of the Word end up deceiving themselves.

We cannot separate our communication of God's Word from our participation in God's work. We must live what we preach. We must walk the walk, not just talk the talk. If we want to preach it, we must be willing to do it.

And finally, remember that our ultimate teacher is the Holy Spirit and the ultimate leadership manual is the Bible. If you're filled with the Holy Spirit and if you read your Bible, then you're moving in the right direction.

The next step of our leadership-development strategy is impartation, and we will discuss it in the next chapter.

DISCUSSION QUESTIONS X

1. Talk about a sermon, teaching, or conference message that changed your life.
2. Talk about a time when you were rebuked or corrected. Did it have a positive or negative effect on your life? Why?
3. Talk about a book that made an impact on your life and ministry.
4. Of the top sources of instruction (classroom instruction, Sunday sermons, personal study, and good books), which one is easiest for you? Why? Which one is hardest? Why?

8

IMPARTATION

*In everyone's life, at some time, our inner fire goes
out. It is then burst into flame by an encounter
with another human being. We should all be
thankful for those people who rekindle the
inner spirit.*

ALBERT SCHWEITZER
Theologian, Philosopher, Physician

*A man cannot impart the true feeling of things
to others unless he himself has experienced what
he is trying to tell.*

JACK KEROUAC, Novelist, Poet, Painter

*For I long to see you, that I may impart to you
some spiritual gift to strengthen you . . .*

ROMANS 1:11

When it comes to impartation, a lot of nutty
teaching is out there, and as is always the case,
bad doctrine leads to weird behavior. In fact,
just today, I received an unsolicited e-mail from a Christian
publication that promised an "impartation" from a world-
famous preacher. All I had to do to get this life-changing
impartation was to simply click and order whatever they

were selling. I didn't bother to click or order, so I guess I missed my impartation opportunity.

Just because unscrupulous religious hucksters attempt to sell an "impartation of the anointing," it doesn't mean we should ignore the subject altogether. Rather, we should search the Scriptures to ensure that we believe and practice only what the Bible teaches about impartation. That's what this chapter will attempt to do.

When I say that impartation is a vital part of our leadership-development strategy, I'm not saying that it's a magical quick fix for spiritual maturity or character development. Ministry would be a lot easier if spiritual maturity could be imparted by having a self-proclaimed apostle lay hands on us at the end of a revival meeting. And wouldn't it be nice if character development could happen instantly by sending "a mandatory freewill love offering" to the famous preacher on the television screen?

But that's not how God designed it.

MORE VALUABLE THAN MONEY

By January 1990, the mission organization that sent Deborah and me to the Philippines had decentralized, disbanded, and/or self-destructed, depending on your perspective. Which of these three terms best described reality didn't matter to us. All that mattered was that six years after Deborah and I became accidental missionaries, reluctant leaders, and clueless church planters, we suddenly found ourselves all alone on the other side of the planet. Plus, when our mission's mother ship sank back in the United States, most of our financial support immediately sank with it. Our church in Manila continued to grow in size, strength, and influence, but our financial base was shrinking fast.

Even though our sending ministry vanished, Deborah and I never doubted our call to make disciples, train leaders, and plant churches in the Philippines—our mission was crystal-clear.

During that time, I instinctively knew that even if we had all the financial partners we needed, something was still missing. Financial provision is important, but certainly not all that we need to accomplish the mission of God. Along with financial partners, I needed mature leaders in my life. I needed someone to encourage me, strengthen me, train me, and mentor me. If I had the right people in my life, then even without adequate funding, I felt everything would ultimately be okay.

I'm so thankful that God brought Emanuele Cannistraci (a.k.a. Pastor C) into our lives and ministry at just the right time. And I'm eternally grateful that Shirley Cannistraci (a.k.a. Sister C) was also part of the deal.

Pastor C was from Northern California but spent most of his time away from his local church, traveling the world preaching the gospel and strengthening pastors. At home, he was Pastor C. All over the world, he was Apostle C. To Deborah and me, Emanuele and Shirley Cannistraci were friends, even though they were thirty years older than us.

Over the years, Pastor C and Shirley ministered at our church and to our leaders many times. In 1990, a few months after our mission organization imploded, seeing that we were clueless and alone, Pastor C took us under his wing and treated us like we were part of his own staff. He mentored us—teaching us by example how to do ministry with integrity, how to do life with joy, and how to do family with no regrets.

Starting in the late 1980s, for over a decade, Pastor C and Shirley made an annual visit to Manila. And every year during that time, their home in San Jose was our first stop on our annual summer visit to the States. It would take another book for me to write all the lessons we learned about life and ministry from Pastor C and Shirley, but consider the pages in this chapter the tip of the iceberg of their impartation.

When our sons were eight, six, and four, we were doing our annual "flash card prep" for our summer trek to the States to visit churches, financial partners, and family. Preparation included holding up a photo and William, James, and Jonathan racking their brains trying to match a name with the face.

> Me: "Who is this guy with the bald head and the white beard like Santa?"
> Jonathan: "I know! That's Papa Jim."
> Me: "And do you know who Papa Jim is?"
> James: "I know. He's your dad."
> Me (holding up another photo): "Anyone know who these people are?"
> William: "That's Uncle Nick and Aunt Juju. They're Mom's uncle and aunt from Georgia."

This process went on for another dozen or so photos of relatives. They missed a few, but they hadn't seen any of them since last year, so I didn't expect them to score a hundred percent. Eventually, they recognized enough of their Mississippi and Georgia relatives for me to end the session. As I was putting the photos away, the following conversation took place:

> William: "Hey, wait a minute, what about our relatives in California? You forgot to show us pictures of them."

Me: "William, we don't have any relatives in California. Only in Mississippi and Georgia."

William: "Yes we do, you know, they are kind of like grandparents, and we always stay in their house when we go to California."

Me: "Oh, you're talking about Pastor C and Miss Shirley, right?"

William: "Yeah, those relatives."

Me: "William, Pastor C and Miss Shirley are not our relatives."

They were not our relatives, but they treated us like family anyway. And in the process of staying in their house, hosting them in Manila, and traveling to the Philippine provinces with them to do ministry, their impartation to our family was transformational in many ways.

Today, Pastor C is eighty-four years old and still circles the globe preaching the gospel and mentoring next-generation leaders. His body is not cooperating all the time, but his mind is sharp, his faith is strong, and his kingdom passion burns hotter than ever.

Hanging out with him for a few days last week (January 2016) strengthened my faith, stretched my vision, and reignited my passion for Jesus. It's difficult to explain, but that's what I mean by impartation.

I hope I'm still making disciples, honoring God, and mentoring next-generation leaders when I am his age.

IMPARTATION IN THE BIBLE

Depending on your preferred translation, the actual words "impartation" or "impart" only appear about a dozen times in the Bible, but stories and examples of impartation appear in both the Old Testament and the New Testament. Here are three well-known examples of impartation in the Bible.

- **Moses and the Seventy Elders.** The word "impartation" isn't mentioned in this story, but it is nevertheless a good example of impartation in a next-generation leadership context.

Then the Lord said to Moses, "Gather for me seventy men of the elders of Israel, whom you know to be the elders of the people and officers over them, and bring them to the tent of meeting, and let them take their stand there with you. . . . And I will take some of the Spirit that is on you and put it on them, and they shall bear the burden of the people with you, so that you may not bear it yourself alone." (Numbers 11:16–17)

Moses did what God said to do; he gathered the people and the seventy elders. He explained what the Lord had instructed him to do. Then he:

. . . gathered seventy men of the elders of the people and placed them around the tent. Then the Lord came down in the cloud and spoke to him, and *took some of the Spirit that was on him and put it on the seventy elders.* And as soon as the Spirit rested on them, they prophesied. But they did not continue doing it. (Numbers 11:24–25)

Impartation is when God takes some of the Spirit that is on one leader and puts it on another. Notice the immediate result of impartation: they prophesied. Also, notice that they didn't continue in this prophetic anointing. In other words, impartation without ongoing discipleship results in a temporary prophetic anointing.

- **Paul and Timothy.** Paul instructed his young protégé, Timothy, "Do not neglect the gift you have, which was given you by prophecy when the council of elders laid their hands on you" (1 Timothy 4:14). Timothy had a gift that was imparted to him by God, through the prophetic ministry of the elders when they laid hands on him, probably during his ordination ceremony. In his second letter to Timothy, Paul reminded him to "fan into flame the gift of God, which is in you through the laying on of my hands . . ." (2 Timothy 1:6). Again, we see that Timothy had a spiritual gift inside of him. Spiritual gifts are ultimately from God, but they're sometimes imparted to leaders through the laying on of hands.

- **Paul and the Church in Rome.** Paul had never visited the church in Rome when he wrote, "For I long to see you, that I may *impart* to you some spiritual gift to strengthen you . . ." (Romans 1:11). Though he hadn't personally met them, Paul instructed them from a distance via the sixteen chapters of the book of Romans. Instruction doesn't require a personal relationship or close proximity to be effective. It can happen through a letter. Impartation requires both a relationship and face-to-face time together. Paul needed to meet them, see them, and talk to them in order for impartation to have its full impact. What did Paul expect impartation to do for the Romans? First, he said he would impart "some spiritual gift" to them. Then Paul said that impartation would make them strong.

In summary, impartation requires close proximity because it transfers spiritual gifts and it makes us strong. It's common to meet leaders who have had plenty of excellent instruction but are still spiritually and emotionally weak. Weak leaders need biblical instruction and impartation. Instruction was never designed to be a stand-alone leadership-development strategy. Instruction and impartation work together to produce leaders who have sharp minds and strong hearts.

FORMING THE HEART

We've seen it in the Bible, but what is it? The word "impart" comes from a Middle English word that means "to give a share of" something to another person. The modern *Webster's Dictionary* tells us that to impart is to "give something" or to "make something known to someone."

Emanuele and Shirley Cannistraci certainly "made something known" to us. Through time spent in their home, whether they knew it or not, they were "giving something" to us. In other words, they imparted faith, hope, love, passion, vision, and other qualities to us, without ever teaching or preaching those topics.

Here are some sample sentences that *Webster's Dictionary* gives to help explain the elusive meaning of this word. "Her presence *imparted* a sense of importance to the meeting." Here's another one: "The oil *imparts* a distinctive flavor to the sauce."

In the Bible, the word "impart" is not some weird mystical phenomenon. Rather, it's as normal as olive oil adding flavor to a sauce or a person's presence upgrading the importance of a meeting.

In our leadership-development strategy, imparta-tion focuses on shaping character, habits, priorities, and values. If instruction is focused on *informing the mind,* then impartation is focused on *transforming the heart.* If the typical setting for instruction is the classroom or the library, the typical setting for impartation is everywhere that real life happens.

Concerning the difference between impartation and plain old discipleship, there is significant overlap. In fact, some of the stories I tell in this chapter to illustrate impartation in our leadership-development context could easily pass as examples of good discipleship and mentoring. However, the distinction between the two is that impartation (as we are using the term here), isn't primarily about helping someone become a better Christian; it's about helping the disciple become a better leader.

What this means in a training context is that while the relationship between the established leader and the emerging leader will touch on many issues that come up in general discipleship, it focuses primarily on issues that relate to leadership and ministry.

This is an important distinction to make because people too often assume that basic discipleship is all that someone needs in order to succeed as a leader. Basic discipleship is the foundation and the starting point for leadership—but emerging leaders will need more input from established leaders in order to succeed. In other words, it's true that leaders need to be discipled, but they also need to be mentored, equipped, and empowered to lead. They need instruction and impartation from established leaders. They need to learn how to respond correctly to difficult leadership scenarios. They need to learn how to balance life and ministry. They need to learn how to treat those they're leading with kindness and respect.

I feel particularly strong about the importance of impartation in leadership development because leaders set the culture of their sphere of influence. For better or for worse, the condition of the heart will affect the people they are leading. Thus, it's vitally important that established leaders develop healthy mentoring relationships with emerging leaders so that they can impart wisdom and shape the character, habits, and values of the young leader.

UP CLOSE AND PERSONAL

We can receive instruction from someone on another continent through online learning platforms, but impartation requires close proximity. We can receive instruction from someone we've never met in person by listening to a podcast, but impartation works through relationship. We can receive instruction from dead people through books, but impartation typically requires a person who's alive right now.

What I've learned about preaching from Charles Spurgeon has been extremely helpful. But there's a profound difference between the preaching instructions found in a Spurgeon book and the preaching impartation I received through being mentored by Pastor C. Both instruction and impartation are necessary for healthy leadership development.

Impartation, as we define it in this book, is inherently relational. And it primarily happens in up-close-and-personal relationships between established and emerging leaders.

As previously mentioned in this chapter, Paul recognized that while his written instruction was important and could happen from a distance, he would not be able to do certain things for the church in Rome until he could be with them in person. We often think about Paul's ministry impact in reference only to his teaching and instruction. It's easy to do so because Paul wrote many letters of instruction that form a significant portion of the New Testament and often those who read Paul's letters had never met him. And these letters of instruction were vital to the health and growth of the local church and its leaders. That's why Paul never hesitated to send instruction to leaders and to churches from a distance. But also, whenever possible, Paul traveled great distances, often risking his life, in order to have face-to-face moments of impartation.

Besides giving general impartation to church congregations, Paul regularly had upcoming leaders travel with him on his missionary journeys. The reason for this traveling mission team was two-fold. First, Paul needed help, so he recruited young missionary interns to accompany him. And second, these young leaders needed help, so Paul allowed them to travel with him to gain the impartation necessary for effective leadership.

Whether in the first century or the twenty-first century, young leaders need impartation from established leaders. And it's up to established leaders to build the necessary relational bridges to speak truth into the emerging leader's life. Relationships of this nature are difficult to build, but they're vital to the leadership development of young leaders.

Impartation is needed, and it can only come from a healthy, life-giving relationship between established and emerging leaders.

WHAT ARE YOU IMPARTING TO FUTURE LEADERS?

So what do we learn in person about leadership that we can't learn in a classroom? What areas of leadership require impartation to accompany instruction? Here are the top six areas where impartation, along with instruction, helped my leadership get to the next level.

1. **Faith.** I have spent more time studying faith than almost any other Bible subject. As a young cross-cultural missionary and church planter, I constantly listened to faith cassette tapes (ancient podcasts) and read faith books. Regular faith infusions were vital to my survival. As helpful as the books and tapes were to build my faith, impartation from four friends took the instruction to another level.

My first faith impartation came from my friend Rice Broocks, who always seemed to have a positive Bible answer to every ministry obstacle. During our college days when my knee-jerk reaction would be to accept a closed door, Rice's reaction was to speak faith and claim a promise from the Bible. The more I hung around Rice, the more the Holy Spirit rebuked my doubt and unbelief, and the more Rice's faith seemed to be imparted to me.

About the same time God was using Rice to provoke me to faith, Phil Bonasso came along and added fuel to the fire. While Rice's faith impartation usually came with high volume and extreme urgency, Phil's faith impartation was mellow and never in a hurry. While Rice's faith impartation always included quoting or praying Bible promises, Phil's faith impartation usually came in the form of funny stories and amazing testimonies.

God used Rice and Phil to impart faith to me during the formative years of Victory and Every Nation. And while they still encourage and strengthen my faith today, no one has imparted more faith to me in the past fifteen years than my friends Joey Bonifacio and Juray Mora. No matter how big the vision, Joey will always challenge me to think bigger. And no matter how big the problem, Juray always reminds me of God's love and His ability and willingness to work it out for my good and His glory.

God used many Bible teachers to inform my head about faith, but He used Rice, Phil, Joey, and Juray to transform my heart through face-to-face impartation.

2. Generosity. Despite an abundance of teaching on tithing, giving, and generosity, many church people don't tithe or give generously. Instruction about giving is obviously not transforming people into generous and joyful givers. That's because instruction must be paired with impartation to have its full effect. Too often, our heads know what to do, but our hearts don't want to do it. Remember, instruction informs the head, and impartation transforms the heart. We need both, especially in the context of generosity.

A pastor can teach and preach about generosity, but without providing an example of generosity, the heart of generosity will be missed. Long before I ever heard biblical instruction about generosity, my parents provided an example of generosity that shaped my heart. Even when they had little money, they were generous. Most generous people I know aren't generous because their heads have been informed; they're generous because their hearts have been transformed. That's the power of impartation.

In the early years of Victory Manila—when we were small and our staff was very young—an older wealthy couple in the church hosted a large party and invited our full-time staff. The party had a lavish spread and an all-you-can-eat buffet, which was rare in Manila in those days. Shortly after the buffet line opened, I noticed that several of our staff members had piled their plates as high as gravity would allow. No part of their plate was visible, just a huge pile of food that required a balancing act to get it safely from the buffet to their table. Most of our staff members were fresh college graduates and didn't have much money, but they certainly weren't starving. The way they acted that evening, you would have thought they were having their last meal before a forty-day fast.

I was surprised and embarrassed by that scene, so I brought it up at our next staff meeting. Most of them didn't understand why I was bothered. What did buffet line etiquette have to do with being a good pastor?

I explained: "We live in a nation that's marked by a poverty mentality—the mindset that 'there's not enough and there will never be enough, so make sure to take as much as you can whenever you can.' How can we break the poverty mentality in our people when we are captive to it ourselves?"

Eventually, they got my point, and we never had an episode like that again—at least with those staff members. However, my goal was not just to break the poverty mentality, but to inspire our leaders to a lifestyle of generosity, no matter how much or how little they had. Leaders need to be openhanded people not only for their own sake, but for the sake of the people who follow them. As leaders, we should be the most generous people in our churches. We probably won't be the wealthiest, but nothing is stopping us from being the most generous.

Are you generous? Do you model a lifestyle of generosity and impart generosity to emerging leaders?

3. Trust. In a previous book, *WikiChurch*, I told the story of my surprise fortieth birthday party. As is often the tradition at Filipino birthday parties, several people took the mic to say something nice about me as the birthday celebrant. Joey Bonifacio spoke first, and much to my surprise, he didn't say anything about my preaching, discipleship, or leadership. Rather, what had made the most impact on him was the fact that I believed in him and entrusted him with large ministry responsibilities. As soon as Joey finished, several other Victory pastors expressed gratitude and amazement that I had trusted them when they were young and unproven.

Throughout this book, I've mentioned several stories related to building trust. Whether it was asking Jun Escosar to lead the Rock Seminar in 1986 or asking Ariel Marquez to lead the Alabang congregation in 2002, both of these men commented that, at the time, they were shocked I had asked them—that I trusted them that much. And they both commented that the confidence I showed in them was empowering, helping them believe that they could bear the seemingly massive leadership responsibility.

The longer I've been in leadership and worked with leaders from other churches and movements, the more I've become convinced that cultures of trust are the best environments to develop strong leaders. As established leaders, we must be willing to let go of control. We must be willing to let young leaders make mistakes. We must be willing to train them and trust them—and get out of their way.

A culture of trust is not easy to build. But know that the decisions you make as a leader will either build or destroy a culture of trust among your emerging leaders. You may not realize it, but your emerging leaders will know instinctively by your leadership practices whether or not you trust them.

Trust is one of those elusive things that is more caught than taught. In other words, it happens primarily via impartation, not instruction.

4. Honor. Established leaders often get credit for good things that happen in and through their church. How leaders handle honor either builds or destroys a leadership-multiplying culture. Early on in my leadership development, I learned that honor is never to be sought and always to be deflected. When deflecting honor, we deflect it in two directions—to God and to the rest of the team.

The first words of our Every Nation mission statement should serve as a constant reminder that the honor that comes from success in ministry is not ours but ultimately God's—for "We exist to honor God . . ." If you're not doing what you do as a leader for His honor, then you've completely missed the point.

I've also found that it's important for established leaders to not only deflect honor to God but also to deflect honor to the rest of the team. Honest leaders know that most of the credit they get for success really belongs to the whole team, not to the senior leader alone.

Success in ministry is a dangerous thing for leaders because it can deceive them into thinking that they did it on their own. Therefore, deflecting honor to others on the team is not only an honest acknowledgement of reality, but a safeguard against the self-delusion.

Remember: any success that you have as a leader comes from the collective effort of your team.

As the leader, you will always get more credit than you deserve. You will also get more than your fair share of the blame when things don't turn out as good as advertised. Learn to embrace the blame and to deflect the honor. Doing so will guard your heart against pride and encourage your developing leaders.

Do you give credit to emerging leaders on your team when things go well? Do you brag about them privately? Do you brag about them publicly? Or do you take all the credit and pass all the blame?

5. Compassion. To have compassion is to care about people, to be sensitive to their hopes, fears, dreams, and needs. Perhaps the most famous compassion story in the Bible is the Parable of the Good Samaritan, a story about two religious leaders who were callous toward the man in the ditch and a despised Samaritan who demonstrated compassion that ended up costing him time and money. (See Luke 10.)

Leading organizations and meetings is much easier than leading people. Organizations and meetings don't require compassion. People do. Organizations don't get their feelings hurt and meetings never rebel. But people often do both. People, even people in leadership positions, are sensitive and insecure and often take things too personally. I know, because I'm a person who leads, and I do all of the above.

When I was new to ministry, I was surrounded by relatively young leaders who were well-meaning, but who sometimes were rather mean to people. While I'm solely responsible for my own leadership sins, I'm pretty sure some unhealthy leadership methods were imparted to me because of close proximity to bad examples. The instruction was biblically solid, but the example was less than Christlike.

As I matured as a leader, I realized that it wasn't enough to effectively lead an organization. I also had to learn to lead people because, after all, Jesus didn't die for an organization or a meeting; He died for people.

Thankfully, the impartation I received from Pastor C and other kind and gracious leaders helped reverse the angry leader within me. It enabled me to have love and compassion toward all people, especially the future leaders I have the privilege of mentoring.

6. Wisdom. I can't think of anything that is more valuable to give to the next generation of leaders than wisdom.

The last chapter of Deuteronomy records the death of Moses and his final impartation to Joshua. Here's the context. First, God took Moses to the top of Mount Nebo and "showed him all the land" (Deuteronomy 34:1). Next, God reminded Moses that He promised to give it to the next generation. Then, Moses died and was buried in an unmarked grave.

Then, it was Joshua's turn to lead. He was ready because of that final valuable gift that was imparted by Moses: "And Joshua the son of Nun was full of the spirit of wisdom. . ." (Deuteronomy 34:9).

Joshua had wisdom. Ultimately, we get it from God, but I'm sure he also gained much wisdom by hanging out with Moses and observing his leadership. I am thankful for the impartation of godly wisdom that I got from my mentors.

These six areas of impartation are just the starting point. The list could include dozens of other areas where we need more than instruction, where we need impartation to multiply strong leaders. In order to become mature leaders, young leaders need impartation as much as they need instruction because we teach what we know, but we impart who we are.

DISCUSSION QUESTIONS X

1. What happens if we get instruction without impartation? What happens if we get impartation without instruction?
2. Are people strengthened or drained when they are around you? Why?
3. Are the decisions you're making building or destroying a culture of trust with your team? Why?

9

INTERNSHIP

My job is not to be easy on people. My job is to take these great people we have and to push them and make them even better.

STEVE JOBS, Apple Cofounder

Practice is the hardest part of learning, and training is the essence of transformation.

ANN VOSKAMP, Author

And he said to them, "Follow me, and I will make you fishers of men."

MATTHEW 4:19

In 1975, I was a sixteen-year-old high school student who had no interest in church, religion, or God. Ron Musselman was the new youth pastor at First Presbyterian Church who graciously, aggressively, and constantly presented the gospel to me. At first I feigned interest, hoping he would go away. When that strategy didn't work, I became slightly antagonistic. This behavior only seemed to encourage him, so I quickly shifted to indifference. After six months of unsuccessfully trying to avoid Ron, I finally gave up and surrendered. Looking back, I'm not sure if I surrendered to Ron or to Jesus, but at some point as I attended Ron's discipleship group, I gradually understood and embraced the gospel.

Five months later, I found myself at a spring break retreat with a hundred teenagers. I'm sure that the retreat had the usual youth group games and activities, but all I remember is the teaching. There were sessions explaining the gospel, grace, faith, and repentance. Other instruction covered Bible basics and devotional prayer. These sessions were theologically rich and extremely practical. It seemed like I gained several years' worth of spiritual growth in one week.

Two sessions had an immediate impact on me. One was on evangelism and the other on apologetics. I had never heard of apologetics, but forty years later I still remember the workshop title, "How to Get His Foot Off Your Neck and Into His Mouth." I am sure no one would use that title today, but the content was solid. This apologetics instruction answered questions that I didn't even know how to articulate. As I listened, I wished the clock would slow down so the session would not end. I resented the breaks, games, and activities. I wanted as much Bible instruction as possible.

But as I've said repeatedly in this book, while instruction is a great starting point, it's not a standalone solution for spiritual growth and leadership development. I needed impartation to go along with the excellent instruction I was receiving. Fortunately, impartation was also available. The more I hung around Ron, the more I caught his burden and compassion for the lost. As they say, some things cannot be taught—they must be caught. I caught so much from Ron in the first few months of my spiritual journey. Some lessons were learned by listening to Ron's teaching and observing his example. Other lessons were caught just by hanging around him.

Because of the teaching at the retreat, I had a rudimentary understanding of how to preach the gospel to friends and family. Because of Ron's example, my heart was broken for the lost, and I actually cared about people who were far from Christ. I knew I was not an evangelist, but I was definitely supposed to be a witness for Christ. So as soon as I got back to school after the retreat, armed with excellent instruction and with a heart filled with compassion for my lost classmates, I now set out to convert my high school.

Fail.

Contrary to the promise of the workshop title, I was never able to "get his foot off my neck and into his mouth." My feeble attempts at being a witness always seemed to end up with both my feet on my own neck and in my own mouth. Instruction and impartation without internship left me feeling like a failure as a witness.

ON-THE-JOB TRAINING

A few months later, at the First Presbyterian summer retreat near a beach in central Florida, Ron and his team presented what they called on-the-job training (OJT), then paired new believers like me with veteran Christians, and we went to parks and beaches to share our faith with random strangers. While I do not recommend approaching unsuspecting strangers as your go-to evangelism method, it did serve as an excellent on-the-job training exercise for the teenage version of me.

Ron's theological instruction had *informed my head*. His compassionate impartation had *transformed my heart*. Now his practical internship was *forming good ministry habits* that would enable me to be an effective witness for Christ.

Eight years later, Deborah and I landed in Manila, and for the next two decades, I basically did what Ron taught me. I used instruction, impartation, and internship to *inform* minds, *transform* hearts, and *form* habits in the future leaders of our church.

I'll never forget the first time I took Ferdie Cabiling on the University of Santo Tomas (UST) campus for OJT evangelism. We were using *The Two Question Test*, which was a simple and effective evangelism tool in the 1980s. At the time, Ferdie was a second-year engineering student at Adamson University.

Though Ferdie was a passionate young man who had been involved in lively student protests against the Marcos regime, he also had a very shy side that manifested in one-on-one situations. As a result, he was initially hesitant to share his faith on campus, so I asked him to come along with me one day.

As we walked around the four-hundred-year-old college campus, I said: "See that guy over there? I'm going to ask him some questions and try to present the gospel. You watch me this time, and you can talk to the next guy."

So Ferdie watched me engage a young UST student with the gospel through *The Two Question Test*. That student attentively listened to my gospel presentation and my personal testimony. He asked a few sincere questions, then had to go to class. After he walked away, Ferdie and I said a short prayer for him.

"Now it's your turn," I said. "You talk to the next guy, and I'll watch and silently pray as you preach the gospel."

I don't remember if anyone received Christ that day, but I know that the experience was vital for Ferdie's development as a leader. He certainly wasn't the only new disciple I took on campus with me to preach the gospel. I think I took just about everyone with me back then. I hoped that people would get saved when we presented the gospel, but what was equally important for me was that our young disciples and emerging leaders were gaining valuable ministry experience.

As the semester went on, Ferdie continued to accompany me to campuses to preach the gospel. He gradually became more and more confident and competent in sharing his faith—so much so, I soon didn't have to ask him to go with me to the campus. He went on his own and brought other young students with him.

By Ferdie's senior year, he was practically a member of our staff—our resident evangelist. We just weren't paying him yet. His leadership in this area was only further developed when I asked him and Jun to lead the Rock Seminar (mentioned in a previous chapter)—an opportunity which, as you know, was not only a surprising success but served as a major turning point in both of their leadership trajectories.

After Ferdie graduated in 1988, we brought him on staff as a campus evangelist and later, as a youth pastor. Eventually, he became my associate pastor, helping me plant several new congregations in Metro Manila over the years. In 2007, after being on staff for nearly twenty years, Ferdie finally agreed to become the senior pastor of Victory Ortigas, our original mall congregation that grew from 2,000 to over 7,000 in weekly attendance under his leadership.

Today, Ferdie is one of the finest leaders I know. He currently serves as the executive director of Victory Manila, overseeing a staff of 422 people, including 110 pastors. He also leads over 10,000 small-group leaders and interns, 137 weekend worship services, and twenty-five Metro Manila locations. More than thirty years ago when I first met Ferdie, he was a young, shy teenager from the province who had no idea that he would one day lead a church of tens of thousands.

THREE COMPONENTS OF INTERNSHIP

When I think about Ferdie's leadership journey, I'm reminded of the importance of internship in our leadership-development strategy. Even though Ferdie was identified early on as an evangelist and received good instruction and impartation over the years, he still remembers our OJT visits to UST in the 1980s as foundational to his leadership development.

Why? Because that's where he gained the initial practical experience needed to develop his gifting and calling as an evangelist. It was a time for him to watch and learn from someone more experienced before he tried ministry himself. It was a time when he could receive immediate helpful feedback as he learned to use his gift wisely and effectively. It was a time when he could develop skills that couldn't be learned in the classroom.

Identification, instruction, and impartation will continue to happen in the context of an internship, but the most important thing in this stage of development is gaining ministry experience in a healthy learning environment.

In short, an internship is an opportunity to watch, learn, and lead with more experienced leaders. An internship has three components: observation, participation, and evaluation.

1. Observation: watch me lead. One of the most important lessons that a young leader can gain from an internship is the opportunity to watch and learn from more experienced leaders. One of the most important things an established leader can do to equip emerging leaders is to spend time with them and allow them to observe as you lead.

If you're a veteran leader, it's important to understand that you don't always have to instruct and impart to younger leaders. There's a time for instruction and a time for impartation, but there's also a time to go about business as usual—just remember to bring a young, aspiring leader along with you. It might come as a surprise, but your future leaders will likely learn more from watching you lead than from listening to you talk about leadership.

The Bible is full of examples of internship relationships. Consider Moses and Joshua. Moses was called to get God's people out of Egypt. Joshua was called to get them into the Promised Land. As you read their story, you will notice how much time Joshua spent with Moses. Many times, even when it didn't seem like Joshua had a major role in the event or the task at hand, Moses brought him anyway. That's what internship is all about.

For example, when Moses went on Mount Sinai to receive the Ten Commandments, he brought Joshua with him to spend forty days and nights on the mountain with God (Exodus 24:13–18). When Moses went to the tent of meeting to seek direction from God to lead the people, Joshua went with him (Exodus 33:7–11). When Moses asked God to provide quail for the entire nation of Israel, Joshua was with him at the leaders' meeting (Numbers 11:4–30).

As far as we know, Joshua did not have a significant role in any of those events, but he was there—watching and learning from Moses. Do you include emerging leaders in meetings where important decisions are being made? Do you bring young leaders along with you to watch and learn as you lead in different contexts?

When we intentionally include young leaders, even when they are not needed, we create internship moments where they can learn lessons by observation that could never be learned in the classroom.

2. Participation: lead with me. Though observation is vital in internships, one of the most powerful components of an internship is participation—when established leaders actually give emerging leaders the opportunity to lead and learn from experience. If established leaders never give new leaders an opportunity to lead, they will not grow as leaders. They may learn from instruction and observation, but they will not develop as leaders until they're allowed to lead.

Some leadership lessons and skills can only be learned by doing, and internships create opportunities for inexperienced leaders to lead and learn in a safe and healthy environment. More importantly, a more experienced leader is close by, in case anything needs to be adjusted.

The relationship between Paul and Timothy is a good biblical example of internship. Paul first met Timothy during a missionary journey through Asia Minor. After hearing good reports from the believers in Lystra and Iconium about this young leader, Paul asked Timothy to accompany him on some of his mission trips. (See Acts 16.)

In the beginning, it's likely that Timothy spent a lot of time simply watching Paul lead and minister. However, from Acts and the epistles, it becomes clear that Paul eventually began to give Timothy increasing leadership responsibilities. The first time we hear of Timothy actually participating in a leadership role was in Acts 17, when Paul leaves Timothy and Silas in Berea to follow up with the new believers in that city. Another time, Paul sent Timothy ahead of him to Macedonia while he remained in Asia to preach a little longer. (See Acts 19:22 and 1 Corinthians 4:17.)

The New Testament does not give a lot of detail about Timothy's work in those cities. But we do know that Paul continually gave him new leadership opportunities and responsibilities. These experiences prepared Timothy for the responsibility of leading the church in Ephesus, one of the largest and most influential churches in the New Testament.

Clearly, Timothy became a great leader in the early church, but what was vital to his development was not only traveling with Paul and observing him lead, but also participating in the work that Paul was doing.

3. Evaluation: learn with me. Another important component of internship and OJT is evaluation. After emerging leaders have watched and learned, then given it a try themselves, it's crucial that they receive feedback from more experienced leaders.

To some, the word "internship" may conjure images of unsupervised, unpaid menial labor doing insignificant tasks, but that's not what we're talking about here. A healthy internship that multiplies leaders involves current leaders and future leaders working together on tasks that matter. And as the current leader intentionally steps back to make space for the future leader to gain experience, it's important for the current leader to watch and evaluate the future leader's attempts at real-life leadership.

Observation and evaluation are essential because inexperienced leaders usually make multiple mistakes as soon they are given new responsibilities. In a healthy learning environment, youthful mistakes can be more instructive than damaging to the organization. However, if the future leader is not carefully watching and working with the emerging leader in the early stages, numerous leadership-development opportunities might be forfeited.

In fact, if guidance and evaluation are not given during an internship, potential leaders will either grow discouraged at their initial attempts to lead, or they will grow overconfident in small early successes. Either way, empowering young leaders with new responsibilities without giving them feedback will greatly decrease the effectiveness of internships.

When Ferdie and I used to preach the gospel at UST, at first, I was just happy that he was coming along with me to watch. But soon, I encouraged him to participate and begin engaging students himself. Had I just sent him away to preach the gospel and not watched how he was doing it, I would have only been doing half of my job in training him as a leader. He needed observation; he needed participation; but he also needed evaluation and adjustment.

After Ferdie got over his initial timidity around strangers, he became very bold in sharing his faith—so bold that sometimes he would get into fiery debates about the Bible and salvation. I was glad for his boldness, but sometimes, he needed a little guidance: "Ferdie, I think you did a great job there, but maybe you could have spoken that truth with a little more love. I understand that you really want to preach the gospel, but you don't have to tell everyone who doesn't want to talk to you that they will 'burn in hell.'"

Jesus suggested similar adjustments to His disciples. For a season, they simply traveled with Him and watched Him lead. Soon enough though, Jesus got them involved in His work, giving them ministry and leadership responsibility that gradually increased throughout His ministry and even more so after His ascension. However, Jesus didn't just turn the disciples loose to lead and minister without any guidance or oversight.

After equipping, empowering, and sending them out, Jesus always had debriefing sessions when His disciples returned. (See Luke 9:1–2,10.) They reported victories and defeats. They asked questions. He answered their questions, adjusted their attitudes, and rebuked their lack of faith. For the disciples, their three-year internship with Jesus was not just about watching Him do miracles. And it was not just about doing unsupervised ministry. It was about working alongside Jesus and receiving helpful feedback as they tried to do what He had been doing.

ALWAYS IN MENTORING MODE

In 2013, William did extensive interviews with Victory leaders about their development as leaders. Here are some quotes and memories from Filipino leaders about internship or on-the-job training. In the following stories and quotes, you will see that on-the-job training looked different for each leader. Internships, whether formal or informal, must be tailored for individuals based on each person's unique calling, personality, gifts, strengths, and weaknesses.

- **Bishop Manny Carlos.** "Victory leaders took me along to do everything with them—counseling, prayer, evangelism, deliverance, building negotiations, and basketball games." That's internship.

- **Dr. Jun Escosar.** During the interview, Jun recounted his first OJT mission trip with me to Indonesia, where he got pulled into an interrogation room and was almost deported before we even left the airport. I think his problem had something to do with the Indonesian immigration officer thinking he had caught a relative of the infamous Colombian drug lord, Pablo Escobar. It took us a while, but eventually, we convinced the immigration officer that since Jun Escosar was Filipino and Pablo Escobar was Colombian, they were not related. Internship usually involves some type of risk, especially when you're mistaken for a wanted drug dealer.

- **Carlos Antonio.** "At twenty-nine, I was the new communications director for Victory, and I had to give a major rebranding presentation to all the senior pastors. The presentation included our new Victory logo and tagline. My job was to convince the pastors to accept some major changes that would cost quite a bit of money and require new signage in all of our centers. Most of the ideas were from the apostolic team, but they made me do the presentation and made sure I got all the credit when everything turned out well." For Carlos, his OJT internship included throwing him to the sharks (senior pastors) immediately. He survived.

- **Dennis Sy.** "I remember when I was the youth pastor, in between services, my senior pastor would gather young preachers like me and ask how he could improve his preaching. He would also call a meeting while preparing for the weekend services to ask us what we would be preaching, then take down notes during our discussion." Internship includes getting the opinions of younger leaders.

- **Ferdie Cabiling.** "I remember one time, I was kind of harsh. I got frustrated and told this guy he was going straight to hell, then I walked away. My pastor and mentor immediately corrected my attitude in private. Then the next day at our staff meeting, he bragged about me in front of the staff as if I had done everything right." Internship always involves private correction and public praise.

- **Paolo Punzalan.** "Confrontation is an important part of leadership, and our leaders were not afraid to confront and correct us when we needed it." Internship is a great time to observe and bring adjustment in young leaders.

- **Joseph Bonifacio.** "My boss often abruptly and randomly asks leaders to walk or drive with him somewhere to discuss something. If you pay attention, you will always learn something during those unplanned 'walk-with-me' moments between classes and during breaks." Internships are sometimes short, spontaneous learning encounters.

What all of these stories and quotes have in common is the intentionality of engaging inexperienced leaders. If we're always on the lookout for future leaders, and if we are always in mentoring mode, then informal internships can have a huge impact on the leaders around us.

THREE GOALS OF INTERNSHIP

I've been using OJT as synonymous to internship. At this point, it might be helpful to explain what I *do not* mean by internship. Often, in corporate and political worlds, interns are young people who do tedious busy work that real leaders are too important to do. In these situations, an internship is a time to "pay your dues" and "earn your stripes" until you eventually get to do work that really matters.

In our context, internship is the exact opposite of unimportant busy work. It gives young leaders the opportunity to watch, learn, and do important leadership work. In our internship phase, the on-the-job training we do is eternally significant.

Internship can be either formal or informal. I have had informal interns who didn't realize they were interns, and I've had official interns, complete with office hours and job descriptions. Both versions are valid.

No matter if it's formal or informal, official or unofficial, internships in our leadership-development strategy have three goals.

1. **Personal confidence.** Despite great instruction and impartation, too many potential leaders are paralyzed by a lack of confidence. In his letter to the Corinthians, Paul mentioned "the *confidence* that we have through Christ" (2 Corinthians 3:4). Ministry confidence should not be in our training or our titles, but in Christ. Paul goes on to say, "Not that we are *sufficient* in ourselves to claim anything as coming from us, but our *sufficiency* is from God, who has made us *sufficient* to be ministers of a new covenant . . ." (2 Corinthians 3:5–6). The first goal of internship is that young leaders would gain *confidence* to minister as they discover their *sufficiency* in Christ.

2. **Professional competence.** While these internship principles can be applied to leadership development in a variety of vocations, they were primarily designed for vocational ministers. Professional competence for vocational ministry leaders starts with knowing God's Word. An early

church leader named Apollos was described as "an eloquent man, *competent in the Scriptures*" (Acts 18:24). Paul, ever instructing Timothy, wrote: "All Scripture is breathed out by God and profitable for teaching, for reproof, for correction, and for training in righteousness, that the man of God may be complete, equipped for every good work" (2 Timothy 3:16–17). God's Word makes us complete and ready for the good work of ministry. Competency in the Word is our second internship goal.

3. Relational connection. Our third goal in formal and informal leadership internship is relational connection. Joey Bonifacio always says, "Discipleship is relationship." I agree, and I believe that the best leadership is also relational. The Bible confirms the importance of relationships, especially in a ministry and leadership context.

> Two are better than one, because they have a good reward for their toil. For if they fall, one will lift up his fellow. But woe to him who is alone when he falls and has not another to lift him up! Again, if two lie together, they keep warm, but how can one keep warm alone? And though a man might prevail against one who is alone, two will withstand him—a threefold cord is not quickly broken. (Ecclesiastes 4:9–13)

Ministry internships and on-the-job ministry training are great avenues for developing deep relationships.

TRAVEL AGENT OR TOUR GUIDE?

When I think about internships as a principle of leadership development in ministry, I'm reminded of a tour guide I once met named Arie Bar-David. As you can probably tell by his name, he's an Israeli tour guide—a Messianic Jew—who gives biblical history tours in the Holy Land.

I've been on two trips to Israel with Arie as the guide, and I can say that Arie is, hands down, the best tour guide I've ever had. He combines his personal experiences, biblical depth, and knowledge of the land to make biblical study tours unforgettable. After touring Israel with Arie, I cannot imagine touring the country without him. Had I taken the same trip without a guide, relying instead on books and online reviews, I'm sure I would have enjoyed it, but the experience would have paled in comparison to our guided tour with Arie.

Internships work the same way. If developing leaders are given good instruction and impartation, they will probably succeed on their leadership journey. The early stages of the leadership journey are much richer when established leaders walk alongside emerging leaders and serve as guides. This is what an internship is meant to do—give young leaders a guided tour of the leadership journey.

Too often, established leaders would prefer to function as travel agents rather than tour guides. Travel agents tell people how to get to places, but their guidance does not extend beyond the comforts of their own office. Tour guides, on the other hand, give guidance before, during, and even after the journey. They work on the ground, and they lead the way.

First-century Pharisees were travel-agent leaders, sitting in places of privilege and authority and telling people how to live. Jesus even told His disciples to "do and observe whatever they [the Pharisees] tell you, but not the works they do. For they preach, but do not practice" (Matthew 23:3).

Jesus, on the other hand, acted like a tour guide. He led, taught, and set an example for the people. His message was not "listen to me"; it was: "Follow me" (Matthew 4:19). Paul was also a tour-guide leader. His message was: "Follow my example, as I follow the example of Christ" (1 Corinthians 11:1, NIV).

Jesus and Paul didn't just sit in an office telling people where to go and what to do; they set the example and led the way—and people followed. That's biblical leadership. That's the power of internship.

Established leaders must identify, instruct, and impart to emerging leaders, but they must also create internship opportunities for future leaders to watch, learn, and lead with them.

What kind of leader are you? Do you lead like a travel agent or a tour guide? Do you lead primarily with words or actions? Do you lead from an office or pulpit, or do you get involved in real life and lead by example?

Leading with words is a lot easier than leading by example. The problem is, it doesn't work. If you want to be an empowering leader, then get out of the office and get with the people so you can lead by example.

DISCUSSION QUESTIONS X

1. How do you respond to evaluation that includes correction?
2. How has an internship (on-the-job training) helped you become a better leader?
3. What should you do when an intern will not receive correction or adjustment during evaluation?
4. Do you intentionally include future leaders in meetings where important decisions are being made? Do you bring young leaders along with you to watch and learn as you lead in different contexts?

LEAVING A LEADERSHIP LEGACY

10

MULTI-ETHNIC OR MULTI-ETHICAL?

Ethics: rules of behavior based on ideas about what is morally good and bad.
MERRIAM-WEBSTER DICTIONARY

Relativity applies to physics, not ethics.
ALBERT EINSTEIN, Physicist

"They shall teach my people the difference between the holy and the common, and show them how to distinguish between the unclean and the clean."
EZEKIEL 44:23

It was supposed to be one of those "Let's open in prayer" moments at the start of an Every Nation North America strategy meeting, but everyone in the room sensed that it might turn into a real prayer meeting. We had a full agenda, but it could wait. God wanted us to pray.

Brett Fuller, our Every Nation North America regional director, prayed for our North American pastors. Russ Austin prayed for our new church planters. Kevin York prayed for our international missionaries. I prayed for our campus missionaries. Then Phil Bonasso prayed a prayer that none of us will ever forget.

After asking God to heal the fragile race relations in certain American cities, Phil waxed eloquent, "And Lord, we pray you will give us more and more *multi-ethical* churches and campus ministries to help heal our nation."

As soon as Phil said "multi-ethical," everyone in the room simultaneously opened their eyes, smiled, snickered, laughed, then laughed out loud uncontrollably.

"Hey, I'm trying to pray. What happened? What's so funny?" Phil had no idea what he had just prayed.

"Phil, America doesn't need any more *multi-ethical* churches." Russ responded, then we all enjoyed another round of laughter.

Obviously, Phil meant to ask God for *multi-ethnic*, not *multi-ethical*, churches and campus ministries. We hope God ignored Phil's actual request and answered the intended prayer of his heart instead.

Russ was correct in his comment about Phil's prayer. More than enough multi-ethical churches and ministries exist in the United States and the world. Unfortunately, there are not nearly enough multi-ethnic churches and ministries.

The idea of a multi-ethical church was funny in that prayer meeting, but in real life, there's nothing funny about church and ministry leaders who fail to uphold a biblical ethic.

IN SEARCH OF BIBLICAL ETHICS

The last four chapters in this book deal with leaving a leadership legacy. Biblical ethics are the starting point of any legacy worth leaving.

It's so sad when a leader spends a lifetime honoring God, then fails at the end and is thereafter remembered for the momentary failure—rather than for decades of sacrificial service. Sometimes, through humility and the grace of God, a leader who falls achieves restoration and still leaves an honorable legacy.

Understanding, defining, and embracing biblical ethics can prevent many potential leadership falls and fails.

On more than one occasion, I have been in a leadership seminar that included a legacy exercise that involved writing my preferred obituary. While this is not my favorite writing topic, I do get the point. Legacy is about what people remember about us long after we are dead and gone. Forcing us to write it down is perhaps the only way to get busy leaders to slow down long enough to actually think about legacy after death. I can't remember what I actually wrote in those seminars, but being forced to think and write about my mortality was a good thing.

The Bible is filled with stories of leaders who left good and bad legacies.

Absalom, the son of King Solomon, is at the top of the list of leaders who left a bad legacy. A large chunk of chapter 13 of this book is dedicated to the sad story of Absalom, but here's a summary of the legacy he left: "Now Absalom in his lifetime had taken and set up for himself the pillar that is in the King's Valley, for he said, 'I have no son to keep my name in remembrance.' He called the pillar after his own name, and it is called Absalom's monument to this day" (2 Samuel 18:18). I am certain that everyone reading these pages desires to leave a legacy that has more kingdom-impact than a stone monument.

On the other end of the legacy spectrum are leaders who leave a legacy that honors God and actually makes an impact on the world.

Jesus is at the top of the list of leaders who left the best leadership legacy. He did not leave behind a monument, a church building, an organization, or a lot of money. Yet, 2,000 years later, billions of people are part of His legacy. Being God incarnate, Jesus left a legacy that mortal leaders cannot possibly copy. None of us can leave behind forgiveness of sins, salvation, and the Holy Spirit as a legacy. But much of the rest of Jesus' legacy is actually attainable by mortal men—including vision, values, relationships, passion, and an all-consuming mission to change the world.

Over lunch yesterday, I had a conversation with Bishop Manny Carlos of Victory Manila and Pastor Tom Jackson, an American missionary and church planter in Scotland. Tom was in Manila to teach Systematic Theology at our Every Nation School of Ministry. While the word "legacy" was not mentioned, everything we discussed was about the legacy we will leave behind. Manny, Tom, and I discussed Leadership 215 (the theological training material that I mentioned in chapter 7), which Every Nation developed to help equip our pastors, especially those serving in non-Christian nations. These dedicated pastors from Muslim, Buddhist, Hindu, and secular backgrounds are hungry for greater theological and biblical training, but it's sadly often not available or affordable in their nations. Our Leadership 215 team, led by Dr. Jun Escosar, worked diligently to fill the gap with accessible training material.

Manny, Tom, and I feel privileged and humbled that we get to help provide material that has the potential to make an impact on hundreds of thousands of new believers in dozens of unreached nations.

That legacy is more preferable to us than having our names carved in stone.

For leaders who want to live a productive life and leave an honorable leadership legacy, it's essential to develop strong ethics in four areas: ministry, money, morality, and marriage.

MINISTRY ETHICS

Ministry ethics are as basic as good manners. But apparently, some leaders were never taught good manners.

When we first landed in the Philippines in 1984, we rented the Girl Scouts' Auditorium for our nightly evangelism meetings. Monday through Saturday, a marginally talented Christian band from the United States presented a worship concert, followed by Rice Broocks preaching the gospel and calling students to Christ.

The 700-seat auditorium was packed with students almost every night. Hundreds heard the gospel, with many of them surrendering their lives to Christ. But as word about our meetings spread, many churches in the area started sending their youth groups each night. Soon, we had so many church kids, there was little room left for the unchurched.

While some church planters might actually get excited about an auditorium filled with Christians, for Rice and our leadership team, this was something to correct, not celebrate. We knew why God sent us to Manila, and it was not to attract Christian kids from other churches.

I'll never forget the night when Rice Broocks attempted to explain why we had come to Manila. It was at the end of our meeting and, as usual, the auditorium was packed with Filipino students. Here's what Rice said: "We came here to start a church for lost Filipino students. If you are a Christian from a good church, then we hope this meeting has helped you. We also hope you will go back to your church and serve Jesus with your whole heart. But please do not come back here. You are taking a seat that should be for a lost student. We are not here to reach Christians. We are here to reach the unreached. Thank you."

That message was repeated almost every night for the rest of the month-long outreach. Some students went back to their churches with a fresh fire. Others ignored Rice and continued to double-dip at their youth group and at our meetings.

Because of a clear ministry ethic, we did not want to do anything that would hurt the existing churches in Manila. We did our best to respect and support other churches by sending their students back. Also, we tried to follow Paul's example "to preach the gospel, not where Christ has already been named, lest I build on someone else's foundation" (Romans 15:20).

Ten years after that original one-month outreach, I continued to encourage Christians to return to their churches and often explained that Victory is a church primarily for non-Christians, not for Christians.

Over the past three decades, many good Christians have transferred to Victory from other churches, but because of ministry ethics, we have always tried to make sure they leave their former church graciously and honorably. Bottom line: we have done our best to avoid a "sheep-stealing" growth strategy.

Here's another example of ministry ethics or, rather, a *multi-ethical* ministry. For as long as I can remember, our church has started each new year with a week of prayer and fasting. For the past fifteen years, we have provided a devotional guide to help our people seek God during that week.

Ten years ago, our communications director showed me a prayer and fasting devotional guide that was a word-for-word copy of ours from the previous year, but the cover featured the logo of another church from a neighboring nation (exactly where the Victory logo used to be). We never included an author's name on our prayer and fasting manuals, but right under the church logo, this manual had the words, "by Pastor Juan dela Cruz" (not his real name). It was our material and our cover, with another church logo and a false author right on the cover.

At first, I found this bold display of *multi-ethical* ministry to be quite hilarious. Our pastors got a good laugh out of it. In fact, ten years later, our communications team still occasionally jokes about it. But after my initial laugh, I was deeply troubled at the lack of ministerial ethics. How can a pastor with a living conscience photocopy the work of a church in a different nation, replace the original church name with his, and claim that he personally wrote it?

Ironically, if they had asked, we would have given them permission to use our prayer and fasting material for free, as long as they did not sell it for a profit. Throughout the years, many churches all over the world have asked and received permission to use and customize our material. But this was the first time someone copied it, branded it with a different church name, and claimed himself as the author.

About a year after the case of the stolen prayer and fasting devotional guide, our communications director reported another situation of ministry ethics failure. This time, it was a small church in a city in the southern part of the Philippines. It had not only named itself Victory, but had also used our exact tagline, logo, and signage. We don't own the name Victory or the Bible verses that mention the word. Thousands of churches all over the world are named Victory. But this church completely ripped off our name, logo, and motto. They were pretending to be us.

We discovered this *faux* Victory church when a staff member happily reported that her sister was now attending Victory in her hometown. I had never heard of that city and told the staff member that we unfortunately did not have a Victory church there. She insisted that there was indeed a Victory church in this city and within twenty-four hours, showed us a photo of the church sign complete with our name, logo, and mission statement.

When our communications director contacted the church about the situation, the pastor admitted that they had copied our identity. He also said that as soon as they had rebranded as Victory, their church suddenly grew. He praised God for the sudden growth and could not understand why this was problematic for us.

Stolen sheep, stolen material, and stolen identity are obvious violations of ministerial ethics. Leaving a leadership legacy leaves no room for a *multi-ethical* approach to ministry.

MONEY ETHICS

Unfortunately, I could share enough examples of leaders violating money ethics to fill the rest of this book.

For example, Gideon had stellar ministry, moral, and marriage ethics. He had some issues with fear, but ultimately, he overcame and obeyed God. The problem for him came after a big victory.

Judges 8:22–23 shares, "Then the men of Israel said to Gideon, 'Rule over us, you and your son and your grandson also, for you have saved us from the hand of Midian.' Gideon said to them, 'I will not rule over you, and my son will not rule over you; the Lord will rule over you.'" Gideon had a great response to a bad request. But soon, he allowed greed to take root.

Judges 8:24 continues, "And Gideon said to them, 'Let me make a request of you: every one of you give me the earrings from his spoil.' (For they had golden earrings, because they were Ishmaelites.)" Taking an offering for yourself is always a bad move for a leader.

In Judges 8:27, we see that "Gideon made an ephod of it and put it in his city, in Ophrah. And all Israel whored after it there, and it became a snare to Gideon and to his family." When leaders violate biblical money ethics, it always becomes a snare and sometimes, becomes the downfall of that leader.

My ministry mentor, Pastor C, often told me, "Money follows ministry. Give yourself to the ministry, and God will give the money. Never seek money. Seek God. Because money always follows ministry." I believe that when leaders do the ministry God has called them to do, He will provide the money. But when leaders seek money, ministry does not necessarily follow. How many potential leaders delay obeying God's call because they're working toward financial security and then end up not doing ministry? Too many. Disaster usually follows the money seekers.

Here are four biblical principles for financial ethical boundaries. It might be helpful to see these as four walls. If we live within the boundaries of these ethical walls, we will be safe. If we go outside these walls, we will find trouble.

1. **Faith: God is my source.** The starting point for developing safe money ethics is to recognize the source of all money and provision, then to put faith in that source. If a pastor sees his congregation as the source, it is inevitable that he will, at some point, compromise and attempt to please the perceived source of funding. On the other hand, if we see God as our source, then we will live to please Him and only Him. Jesus said, "No one can serve two masters, for either he will hate the one and love the other, or he will be devoted to the one and despise the other. You cannot serve God and money" (Matthew 6:24).

2. **Integrity: the law is my standard.** When I say the law is the standard, I'm referring to the law of God in the Bible and the law that governs your nation. Integrity matters to God and to people. That's why I've given the following speech to our external auditors on multiple occasions:

> I want you to hold our organization to the highest standards—higher than any of your other clients. We are a church and a mission organization; we have an obligation to God and to our financial partners to operate with absolute integrity. We do not believe in financial gray areas.

Paul's philosophy of financial integrity drove him to be right in the eyes of God and man. Here's how he explained his financial policies to the Corinthian church. "We take this course so that no one should blame us about this generous gift that is being administered by us, for we aim at what is *honorable not only in the Lord's sight but also in the sight of man*" (2 Corinthians 8:20–21). Paul's goal was to be "honorable" in the sight of God and man. In other words, our financial guidelines must be twofold: God's Word and man's law. Our starting point is always the Bible, but we must also obey the laws of our nation in order to be honorable in the eyes of man. However, while the general rule is to follow the laws of the land, there are certainly places where the law of the land contradicts the law of God. Integrity demands that we follow the law of God no matter the cost to disobeying local laws. But again, this is the exception. The rule is to follow the law.

3. Wisdom: the team is my safety net. In the early days of Victory Manila, I had to negotiate our first few contracts. But as the church, the budget, the bills, and the risk grew, I knew that I needed to surround myself with a team of smart people that had more experience and more knowledge than me. I knew the Bible, but I did not know Philippine real estate or banking laws. Financial and business wisdom did not mysteriously drop from heaven to me when I needed it. Rather, it came to me as I asked questions and listened to wise people on my team.

To get wisdom from God, I had to admit to myself and to those around me that I was not the smartest person in the room, especially pertaining to legal contracts and financial matters. I knew the mission of God for our church better than anyone else, but I desperately needed financial wisdom. For me, it would have been unethical to make major financial decisions alone without building a great team and listening to their wisdom.

4. Generosity: the money is not mine. Now, for the last and possibly the most important foundation of money ethics: generosity. It would be tragic to see God as my source, to respect the Bible and the law as my standard, and to build a great team of wise financial advisors, only to hoard money. But, sadly, many leaders who have faith, integrity, and wisdom use money only for themselves or their own church. Paul explained the purpose of prosperity to the Corinthian Christians like this: "You will be *enriched* in every way to be *generous* in every way . . ." (2 Corinthians 9:11). The purpose of God's provision is so that we can be generous all the time in every way.

Many years ago, when my three sons were studying at Faith Academy, an international school in Manila, Deborah and I prayed for God's provision so we could prepay their tuition. A significant discount was available for parents who prepaid rather than paid monthly, but we did not have the cash. As I earnestly and desperately prayed for provision, I felt rebuked by the Lord. He was not offended that I was asking Him for so much money all at once. Rather, I felt rebuked for asking for too little. Under the conviction of the Holy Spirit, I felt very selfish for asking God only for the exact amount I needed. It suddenly hit me that if I only believed God for the exact amount I needed, there was no way I could be generous and help others. I repented for thinking only of my needs, and from then on, I have usually doubled my request so I can "be generous in every way." A biblical money ethic is a generous ethic.

MORAL ETHICS

In the previous section, I said that there are plenty of examples of money ethics violations. Sadly, I can think of many more examples of moral ethics violations. King David's fling with Bathsheba is perhaps the most infamous.

The introduction to the David and Bathsheba story hints at the reason for David's fall. In 2 Samuel 11:1, we see that "In the spring of the year, the time when kings go out to battle, David sent Joab, and his servants with him, and all Israel. And they ravaged the Ammonites and besieged Rabbah. *But David remained at Jerusalem.*"

As we've talked about in a previous chapter, when leaders decide not to do what they're supposed to do, trouble is often waiting next door. We aren't told why David sent Joab to do his job, but we know the tragic results. When he should have been leading his army into battle, he was looking at something he should not have been looking at—a naked woman taking a bath. When men look at what they should not look at, they eventually do what they should not do.

After committing adultery, David made it worse by attempting to cover up rather than confessing. Fortunately for David, he had a faithful friend who was willing to confront his sin, and he had a gracious God who was willing to forgive his sin. But he experienced painful consequences. (For the full story, see 2 Samuel 11 and 12.)

Biblical moral ethics begin with the Bible, and the Bible sets high moral standards that should not change from culture to culture or from century to century. Notice the moral standard that Paul expected the Corinthians to adhere to, even though sexual promiscuity was accepted in their culture (1 Corinthians 6:18–20). "Flee from sexual immorality. Every other sin a person commits is outside the body, but the sexually immoral person sins against his own body." Paul did not advise them to stay and fight, but to flee. Many leaders wrestle when they should run.

Paul goes on, "Or do you not know that your body is a temple of the Holy Spirit within you, whom you have from God?" In other words, he reminded them how close the Holy Spirit is to every believer, especially during times of intense temptation.

Paul continues, "You are not your own, for you were bought with a price. So glorify God in your body." As usual, Paul takes it back to the Lordship of Christ and the power of the gospel. "You are not your own" is a summary of Lordship. "You were bought with a price" is a summary of the gospel. The only reasonable response to who He is (Lordship) and what He did (the gospel) is to "glorify God in your body."

Paul did not make up the idea of fleeing from sexual immorality. It was the standard way leaders dealt with temptation for hundreds of years. Perhaps when Paul told the Corinthians to flee, he was thinking about a story from the life of Joseph (Genesis 39:7–23).

Joseph was his father's favorite son. This fact did not sit well with his older brothers, so they decided to kill him. But they had second thoughts when they realized they could sell him into slavery and make some pocket money. After being sold as a slave, Joseph ended up as head houseboy for a rich Egyptian named Potiphar. Pretty soon, Potiphar's wife noticed that "Joseph was handsome in form and appearance." After stalking him for a few days, the Bible says that Mrs. Potiphar "cast her eyes on Joseph and said, 'Lie with me.'" People often lament how forward females are in our modern societies, but I say sin and temptation are the same yesterday, today, and forever.

How should a leader who wants to walk in a biblical moral ethic respond to temptation and invitations to sin? We are told that Joseph "refused" her temptation with these words, "'How then can I do this great wickedness and sin against God?'"

This did not even slow her down one bit. She was determined to force Joseph to violate his moral ethics. "And as she spoke to Joseph day after day, he would not listen to her, to lie beside her or to be with her." Notice that Joseph not only refused to have sex with her, he also refused to be in the same room with her. His moral ethic taught him to avoid temptation.

Paul exhorted the church in Ephesus that "Among you there must not be even a hint of sexual immorality, or of any kind of impurity, or of greed, because these are improper for God's holy people" (Ephesians 5:3, NIV). We are not God's holy people because we live holy lives. We are God's holy people because Christ lived a holy life and died for our sins. Because of what He did for us, and because of who we are in Him, even a hint of sexual immorality is improper.

Living according to a biblical moral ethic includes fleeing from sexual sin—not even being in the same room with someone who is offering an opportunity to sin—and living a life that doesn't have a hint of sexual immorality.

MARRIAGE ETHICS

Again, to develop our ethical boundaries for marriage, we start with the Bible, not with the current ideas of our culture. And the beginning of the Bible is a great place to start.

Thousands of years ago, the big marriage issue was divorce or remarriage. Today, in much of the world, the big marriage issue is same-sex marriage. Jesus answered the divorce question by dealing with the sinful heart of people and by pointing them back to the Genesis pattern.

We should answer the same-sex marriage question the same way—by dealing with the heart and pointing people back to the Genesis pattern.

Adam was perfectly okay being alone with the animals, but God said in Genesis 2:18, "It is not good that the man should be alone." God's solution was to "make him a helper fit for him." Adam's helper was a female and her name was Eve. Notice that God did not make a group of helpers for the man. He made one. God's original intention for marriage was one man and one woman.

The pages of Scripture record many times that sinful men thought they had a better idea and violated God's original one-man-one-woman pattern with multiple wives. Perhaps the most extreme case was Solomon, who reportedly had 700 wives and 300 concubines.

The Bible does not endorse the practice of polygamy; it only reports it. The Bible also does not ignore the practice. In fact, the stories of Bible characters who had multiple wives serve as a clarion call to warn individuals who might be tempted to follow in their foolish footsteps. Read the story of Abraham and his multiple wives or Jacob and his multiple wives (Genesis 15–36), and decide for yourself if polygamy is a good idea.

Marriage was not only designed by God to be between one man and one woman; it was also designed to be for life or "till death do us part." Matthew 19:3–9 records a story of some Pharisees asking Jesus, "Is it lawful to divorce one's wife for any cause?" Notice the question. They were not asking a generic question about divorce. They were specifically asking His opinion about the liberal sect of Pharisees who taught divorce for any and every reason.

Before Jesus answered the specifics of their question, He pointed them back to Genesis. "Have you not read that he who created them from the beginning made them male and female, and said, 'Therefore a man shall leave his father and his mother and hold fast to his wife, and the two shall become one flesh'? So they are no longer two but one flesh. What therefore God has joined together, let not man separate."

After establishing the foundation of God's original plan, Jesus then made it clear that divorce for any and every reason is not God's will. This certainly pleased conservative Pharisees who allowed no divorce for any reason. But the liberals, who did not get the answer they wanted, responded with another question, "Why then did Moses command one to give a certificate of divorce and to send her away?"

Like He often did, Jesus made it a heart issue when He answered, "Because of *your hardness of heart* Moses allowed you to divorce your wives, but from the beginning it was not so." Notice that, after dealing with the heart, Jesus brought the debate back to the beginning in Genesis.

The next words Jesus uttered offended the same conservatives that He had previously pleased. Remember, these conservative Pharisees did not allow divorce ever, for any reason. "And I say to you: whoever divorces his wife, *except for sexual immorality*, and marries another, commits adultery."

I am not attempting to present a comprehensive theology of marriage and divorce in this short chapter. Rather, I'm saying that our marriage ethic must start with God's original pattern in Genesis—one man and one woman. After establishing that foundation, then we must also take into consideration the words of Jesus and the writings of the Apostle Paul on the subject of marriage. What we cannot do is allow the shifting sands of public opinion to move the ancient boundaries that God's Word established.

If we want to develop a marriage ethic the way Jesus did, we need to apply Genesis to current culture. We do not start with current trends and make them fit in with the Genesis account.

If we want to address the multiplication challenge and leave a leadership legacy that will honor God, we will have to understand biblical ethics and establish standards that govern ministry, money, morality, and marriage. These ethical standards are not to restrict us, but to protect us. They are based on eternal Scripture, not temporal fads.

DISCUSSION QUESTIONS X

1. Which of the four areas (ministry, money, moral, marriage) do you find most challenging? Why?
2. Name at least three people whom you have allowed to speak into your life in these four areas. Describe your relationship with them.
3. Personally, what is one area you need to guard? Why?

11

SUCCESSORS
OR SUBORDINATES?

*When we are planning for posterity, we ought to
remember that virtue is not hereditary.*
THOMAS PAINE, Philosopher

*I don't think it is good for the country to have a
former president undermine his successor.*
GEORGE W. BUSH, Former US President

*"'I am the God of Abraham, and the God of Isaac,
and the God of Jacob . . .'"*
MATTHEW 22:32

I get to travel all over the world, and I get to participate
in lots of great conferences, but, year after year, one of
my favorites is our Asia Pastors' Equipping Conference
(a.k.a. APEC). As its name would suggest, APEC is a
gathering of pastors, church planters, and cross-cultural
missionaries who do life and ministry in Asia. The APEC
purpose is twofold: ministry equipping and relational
connection. The equipping is great, but for many of us,

APEC is an excuse to connect with lifelong friends from all over the world.

No matter which city hosts APEC—Singapore, Kuala Lumpur, Bali, Manila—the experience has always been unforgettable and life-changing. APEC 2015 was hosted in Manila in our newly opened Every Nation facility, and included 375 pastors and missionaries from 37 nations.

It was refreshing and inspiring to reconnect with friends from Afghanistan, Bangladesh, Cambodia, China, Laos, Mongolia, Myanmar, Nepal, North Korea, Sri Lanka, Vietnam, and other nations in Asia.

Our 2015 theme was "A Pastor's Key Relationships," and we had an excellent team of teachers scheduled to address various aspects of relational leadership. My friend Jim Laffoon was planning to deliver a message called "Covenant Relationships." A few months earlier at our Middle East Strategic Summit (a.k.a. MESS) in Abu Dhabi, Jim had brilliantly spoken on the topic, so we couldn't wait to have him give the same talk to our Asian leaders. But due to a health issue, Jim had to cancel at the last minute.

It took our Asia regional leadership team one e-mail and a five-minute discussion to decide that Skek Hosoi should be the replacement for Jim's session. Considering the following, it might be difficult for the untrained eye to see why Skek was the perfect replacement for Jim. But to our Asian team, it was an easy choice.

Jim is in his sixties and has been preaching constantly for the past forty-one years. Skek is in his twenties and has been preaching occasionally for the past three years. Jim has a globally recognized prophetic ministry to church, business, and political leaders. Skek ministers to teenagers in his local church in Japan. Jim has written four books. Skek has read some books. Jim stands over six feet tall.

Skek stands over five feet tall. Jim is on the Every Nation International Apostolic Team. Skek is a youth pastor at Every Nation Yokohama. Jim has spoken at hundreds of global conferences. Skek has attended some conferences. Jim is an experienced grandfather. Skek is a new dad. Jim is the son of a pastor. Skek is the son-in-law of a pastor.

That last one was the clincher—not that Skek works with his father-in-law, but that he works as part of a multi-generational leadership team that happens to be led by his father-in-law, Scott Douma. When we told Skek what Jim's topic was, he informed us that he had no idea how to talk about covenant relationships, so he requested to change his topic to "How to Relate to the Next Generation."

While we missed having Jim with us in Manila, Skek's message was one of the highlights of APEC 2015. I wasn't surprised. I expected nothing less from him.

As Skek was speaking on the APEC stage, Scott—his pastor, mentor, and father-in-law—was smiling proudly. At that moment, the Apostle John's words in 3 John 1:4 popped into my head. "I have no greater joy than to hear that my children are walking in the truth." I agree with John's inspired words and Scott's proud smile—there is no joy greater than the joy of watching the next generation of spiritual leaders grow in their leadership capacity.

To everyone who watched Skek humbly and confidently minister to his leaders and peers at APEC, it was obvious that Scott had done a great job preparing the next generation of Japanese leaders for success. The more old leaders prepare future leaders for the task ahead, the more successful they will be.

But how does a leader prepare for the future?

MULTI-GENERATIONAL
LEADERSHIP PREP ESSENTIALS

King David had his ups and downs and made a lot of mistakes, but he got it right when it came to helping his successor succeed. David finished well, not only because of what he personally accomplished, but also because he prepared the next generation for greatness. So many leaders succeed, only to have the next generation destroy what they had worked so hard to build. That's not David's story because he prepared Solomon for the leadership challenges ahead.

Here's how David's story ended. After all he had accomplished as a soldier and king, David had one final vision—to build a magnificent house for the presence of the Lord. Over time, it became clear that God's will was not for David to build God's house. Building a house for God's presence was definitely in God's plan, and it was in David's heart. But it was not for David's generation. Building God's house would be for the next generation. (See 1 Kings 8:17–18 and 1 Chronicles 22:6–10.)

What should a leader do with a vision that's beyond one generation? Some leaders run ahead of God and attempt to do it even though it's not the right timing. Other leaders avoid all vision that they cannot personally accomplish. David did neither. Instead of disobeying God or discounting the vision, David developed the next generation and prepared to fulfill what God had put in his heart.

Everything I have been doing in ministry for the past three decades—making disciples, developing leaders, planting churches, and strengthening campus ministries—was originally in the hearts of the leaders that God used to shape my life and ministry. Somehow those leaders—Ron

Musselman (a Presbyterian youth pastor), Walter Walker (a Mississippi State University campus missionary), Bob Weiner (a global campus mission leader), Emanuele Cannistraci (a friend and mentor), and others—took what God had put in their hearts and imparted it to me. I inherited so much vision from my predecessors that I didn't have to make up any new mission or vision. One of the most elusive parts of leadership is imparting what God has put in our hearts to the next generation. Transferring doctrine, strategy, organizational charts, and systems is easy. Transferring things of the heart is difficult.

As a leader, God has put things in your heart that cannot possibly be accomplished in your lifetime. If this isn't the case and your vision can be fulfilled in your lifetime, then your vision is too small. When God's vision for your life and for your ministry is bigger than you, it requires you to learn to work with, walk with, lead with, and prepare the next generation.

As David transitioned leadership to the next generation, he succeeded where other leaders have failed because he focused on four areas that are essential for healthy multi-generational leadership.

1. People. Knowing that no leader can lead alone, David's first move was to galvanize his team's support for his successor. He "commanded to gather together" various people that he knew Solomon would need to accomplish the vision. He "also commanded all the leaders of Israel to help Solomon . . ." (1 Chronicles 22:2,17). David had a loyal team of people who had partnered with him through thick and thin. They had sacrificed together, fought together, led together, and prospered together. Now, he "commanded" them to partner with the next team leader. If you want the leader who follows you to succeed, then you will need to use your influence to get the right people to partner with him or her. You didn't do it alone, and your successor cannot do it alone. Help your people make the transition to their new leader.

2. Preparation. Getting the "right people on the bus" is an essential first step. The second step is to get the right people to do the right things, and that requires preparation. David didn't get to read the leadership classic *From Good to Great* by Jim Collins, but he definitely understood the lesson that leaders have to "confront the brutal facts, yet never lose faith." First Chronicles 22:5 records two brutal facts David had to face. The first fact was obvious to all: "Solomon my son is young and inexperienced . . ." So many leaders face the reality of next-generation inexperience and mistakenly tighten their grip on the leadership baton. All this does is ensure that the next generation will remain inexperienced. When our Asia team discussed possible replacement preachers for Jim Laffoon's APEC slot, we considered the fact that Skek was young and inexperienced and decided that we would give him a shot anyway.

Here's David's second brutal fact: "the house that is to be built for the Lord must be exceedingly magnificent . . ." The fact that the task is exceedingly huge and the potential leader is exceedingly inexperienced has never bothered God. It didn't seem to bother David either. Notice how David responded to the brutal facts. "I will therefore make preparation for it." The solution to a great task and inexperienced leadership is preparation. But what did David mean by preparation? As we will see in our next point, preparation can be expensive.

3. Provision. Every pastor who has attempted a building program knows that if "the house that is to be built for the Lord must be exceedingly magnificent," then the budget will also be exceedingly magnificent. The verse that tells us about God's magnificent building, Solomon's inexperienced leadership, and David's careful preparation ends with this sentence: "So David provided materials in great quantity before his death." Unlike many pastors, David didn't leave the next generation saddled with building debt, but with finances to build the next phase debt-free. A few chapters later, we get another reminder of Solomon's inexperience and a description of David's generous provision.

> And David the king said to all the assembly, "Solomon my son, whom alone God has chosen, is young and inexperienced, and the work is great, for the palace will not be for man but for the Lord God. So I have provided for the house of my God, so far as I was able . . ." (1 Chronicles 29:1–2)

David did his part with gold, silver, bronze, iron, wood, and other building materials. But he didn't stop there. He challenged everyone else to follow his example of generosity toward the next generation's success—"Who then will offer willingly, consecrating himself today to the Lord?" (1 Chronicles 29:5). Because of David's example of generosity and his exhortation to freely give, notice how the people responded.

> Then the leaders of fathers' houses made their freewill offerings, as did also the leaders of the tribes, the commanders of thousands and of hundreds, and the officers over the king's work. . . . Then the people rejoiced because they had given willingly, for with a whole heart

they had offered freely to the Lord. David the king also rejoiced greatly. (1 Chronicles 29:6,9)

Raising money to build magnificent buildings was new to Solomon, but not to David. The same is usually true today with older and younger leaders. Leaders who want their successor to succeed will help with generous provisions, rather than bind them with irresponsible debt.

4. Prayer. The right people, wise preparation, and generous provision are all essential for multi-generational leadership success. But without God's divine touch, they're all still woefully inadequate. David knew that ultimate success is always in God's hands. After doing everything humanly possible to ensure the success of his successor, David cried out to God with a prayer of humility and thanksgiving. His heartfelt prayer ended with an appeal to God about Solomon's heart. "Grant to Solomon my son a whole heart that he may keep your commandments, your testimonies, and your statutes, performing all, and that he may build the palace for which I have made provision" (1 Chronicles 29:19).

Successful succession ultimately comes down to the heart of the next-generation leader. Perhaps the most important multi-generational leadership lesson from David and Solomon is that no matter the magnitude of inexperience, if the young leader's heart is right before God, all will be well in the end. This is what we were counting on when we replaced the experienced veteran Jim Laffoon with the inexperienced rookie Skek Hosoi. We knew that Skek would probably say something that would have to be edited before the APEC podcast went public, but that didn't matter as long as his heart was right with God. But actually, nothing had to be edited out of Skek's message. On the other hand, as usual, my message required several edits before it was ready for public consumption.

DIRT, DIAMONDS, AND LEADERSHIP DEVELOPMENT

Let me tell you about Skek's message. Day one at APEC 2015 went better than ever. Day two, it was Skek's turn to take the main stage and deliver our keynote message. Scott Douma gave a serious and humorous introduction to Skek. Then after some hilarious back-and-forth trash talking with his father-in-law, Skek took his nervousness in stride and powered through with his message. He introduced his topic by narrating his journey to leadership. He brilliantly contrasted Japan's *sempai/kohai* system, where the younger is expected to remain subservient to the elder, with the Apostle Paul's "fellow worker" philosophy, where the elder and younger work and serve together. It is difficult for non-Asians to completely understand just how powerful hierarchy is in Asian honor cultures. Japan's *sempai/kohai* system takes hierarchical honor culture to the next level that can either be extremely healthy or extremely dysfunctional, depending on the security or insecurity of the *sempai*.

To help us understand his point about the *sempai/kohai* system, Skek flashed two photos on the giant LED screens. The first photo was a familiar scene where four servants carry two parallel poles with an ornate chair sitting on the poles. The leader is seated on the throne-like chair and is carried by the four servants.

The second photo also included four people and a leader, but this time, they were all in a single-file line straining to pull a harness that was attached to a cart. Another ornate chair was on top of the cart, but this time, it was empty. Rather than riding in the cart and being pulled by the servants, the leader was the first one in line. He was not only doing his part to pull the cart, but he was also setting the example for everyone else to follow.

Skek explained that in the first photo, the leader was a burden to the rest of his team. In the second photo, the leader was carrying the burden along with the people he led. The obvious unasked question hanging in the air was, "Are you a burden to those you lead, or do you help carry the burden along with those you lead?"

After an uncomfortable moment (in which 375 leaders silently examined their leadership style, hoping that they were a burden-bearer, not a burden), Skek made another poignant point with a photo on the big screen. This photo featured a mining excavation of some sort, with mountains of dirt surrounding a huge manmade hole and massive machinery digging and removing the dirt. Skek then explained the process of mining diamonds and compared it to the biblical process of developing leaders.

In a best-case scenario, in the world's most diamond-rich mining locations, about one hundred tons of dirt must be removed per carat of diamonds. In the average diamond mining locations, 1,000 tons of dirt yield one carat of diamonds. That's a lot of dirt to remove in order to discover a small number of diamonds. But according to Skek, if we want to find next-generation leaders, we will have to dig and remove lots of dirt.

As we multiply leaders, our job is not to create next-generation leadership diamonds. We don't have the power to create anything. The good news is that God has already created all the leaders we need. The bad news is that they're hiding in the dirt. If we're willing to get our hands dirty, then we'll find plenty of leadership diamonds. But finding a leadership diamond is not the end; it's just the beginning.

Using Skek's analogy, here's how and where Victory finds our leadership diamonds.

First, we decide on a mine or a field. For us, that's primarily the university campus. Then, convinced that diamonds are hidden in the campus dirt, we start digging. Next, we work hard removing dirt (lots of dirt). Eventually, we find a dirt-covered diamond-in-the-rough. After cleaning the dirt off, we cut the rough diamond. Next, we polish and shape it. And finally, we place it in the right setting.

Most strong young leaders are hiding in the dirt of sin. They don't look like leaders at all, but once they're cleaned, cut, polished, shaped, and set, they will sparkle.

All of the future leaders you will ever need are hiding in the dirt. The question is, will you get your hands dirty in order to find, shape, and set them?

HOW TO LEAD WITH NEXT-GENERATION LEADERS

When Barnabas started mentoring Paul, he was certainly a diamond in the rough. Gradually, as God dealt with Paul, the Pharisaical dirt was removed, the racist attitudes were cut off, the leadership and teaching gifts were polished, and Paul was put in the right setting as an apostle to the Gentiles.

When Paul found Timothy, he was also a diamond in the rough, but with different rough parts than Paul had. Where Paul was an overconfident Jewish purist, Timothy was an insecure half-Jew, half-Greek. In the same way God removed Pharisaical dirt from Paul, he removed the Gentile dirt from Timothy. God used Paul to clean, cut, polish, and set Timothy as a next-generation leader.

Paul's relationship with Timothy serves as a healthy example of multi-generational leadership. Unlike the *sempai/kohai* system (or whatever that system might be called in another culture), Paul didn't relate to Timothy as a subordinate, always reminding him of his subservient position beneath Paul. On the contrary, Paul seemed to constantly and intentionally elevate Timothy's role and position by referring to him as a "fellow worker" or a spiritual "son."

If we really want to have strong next-generation leaders coming behind us and working with us, we need to see them and relate to them as God-ordained successors, not as permanent subordinates.

Here are four principles from Paul's relationship with Timothy that might help older *sempai* leaders relate to younger *kohai* leaders.

1. Include them. I'm sure Paul never forgot his early days as a new Christian when no one trusted or included him. He felt the call of God on his life, but he had few open doors for ministry. That all changed when a respected church leader named Barnabas took a risk and shared his ministry platform with the upstart apostle. Barnabas included Paul on his ministry trips and in his ministry plans.

Years later, after he had become a respected theologian and church leader, Paul did the same for young Timothy. He included him when others didn't exactly see Timothy as a leader. Besides Jesus, no name is mentioned in Paul's epistles more than Timothy. Paul not only mentions Timothy in his letters, he includes him in the introductory salutations in 2 Corinthians, Philippians, Colossians, 1 and

2 Thessalonians, and Philemon, indicating that Timothy was a vital part of Paul's leadership team.

Do you include or exclude potential next-generation leaders from significant leadership situations? The more you include them, the better leaders they will become.

2. Trust them. Ananias trusted Paul's conversion story when others weren't so sure. Barnabas trusted Paul to do ministry when others doubted his grace theology. Eventually, Paul became a respected teacher, theologian, and missionary apostle, and he extended trust to potential next-generation leaders in the same way that Ananias and Barnabas had trusted him. Paul gave young Timothy huge ministry responsibilities when others probably would have preferred a more proven leader. I'm sure that being trusted by a great apostle like Paul did much for Timothy's identity and security as a leader.

Here's what Paul said about Timothy to the Philippian church: "For I have no one like him, who will be genuinely concerned for your welfare. For they all seek their own interests, not those of Jesus Christ." Paul then says that Timothy has "proven worth" and that their relationship is "as a son with a father" (Philippians 2:19–22). The fact that Paul sent Timothy on an important mission to Philippi confirmed his trust in his young protégé. Paul's words of trust underlined his actions of trust.

3. Serve with them. As I mentioned in the chapter on acting like a leader, Jesus came to serve the least and taught that real leaders should think and act like servants. All too often, modern leaders expect people to serve them. This convoluted modern leadership model is not unique to the American church. Tragically, the "serve me and one day, you'll be a leader" philosophy is a global problem in the church.

Paul didn't teach a "serve me" pathway to leadership. He taught a "serve *with* me" model. Notice how Paul described his multi-generational leadership relationship with Timothy. "But you know Timothy's proven worth, how as a son with a father he has *served with me* in the gospel" (Philippians 2:22). The key word is "with," not "serve." Paul said Timothy "served with me" and not that "Timothy served me."

Serving a leader is very different than *serving with a leader.* Leaders should raise up other leaders to serve *with* them. If you want weak "yes-men" rather than strong leaders, the best way is to create a culture where younger leaders are expected to serve older leaders. But if you want to raise up strong next-generation leaders, then create a culture where young leaders serve and minister together with older leaders. This requires trust.

4. Father them. Paul often used father and son language to describe his multi-generational leadership model. Particularly in his relationship with Timothy, he referred to Timothy as his "child," his "true child in the faith," and his "beloved child" (1 Timothy 1:2; 2 Timothy 1:2; 2 Timothy 2:1).

Just a caution, though. This "spiritual father" thing can get weird real fast. When leaders demand or expect to be honored or introduced as a "spiritual father" or a "spiritual mother," it's often a sign of insecure and manipulative leadership. I suggest you run away as far and as fast as you can when someone demands to be honored as a "father." Honor is supposed to be freely given, not demanded. I've seen leaders who label themselves "spiritual fathers," then demand honor, authority, and financial support from their "sons." Often these "sons" desire to live honorable lives, but are worn out by the endless and irrational demands of insecure "fathers." When the phrase "spiritual father" is descriptive of reality, then it can be healthy. But when it is demanded, it's dysfunctional. Fathering the next generation means acting like a loving, caring father. It does not mean demanding a title or position.

What it means to be a father changes over time, too. As I write this chapter, my sons are twenty-nine, twenty-seven, and twenty-five-year-old adults. My granddaughter is two years old. As a father, I relate to my twenty-nine-year-old adult son vastly different than the way he relates to his two-year-old daughter. Unfortunately, insecure and confused "spiritual fathers" often treat their adult "spiritual sons" like they're still spiritual toddlers. Don't do that. Healthy fathering means recognizing spiritual maturity and adjusting accordingly.

DON'T PASS THE BATON

My friend, Russ Austin, has taught me much about leading the next generation, and more importantly, about leading *with* the next generation. During the seven years that Russ served as our Every Nation North America Director, our regional leadership team had countless conversations about next-generation leadership.

Russ always argued against using "passing the baton" language, even though most leaders our age seem to be obsessed with it. New blogs, podcasts, conferences, and books about passing the baton are ubiquitous. The pass-the-baton bandwagon is difficult to ignore. But the problem with the pass-the-baton analogy is that many of us are still strong, healthy, full of vision, and not quite ready to retire to the cheering section. We may not be running as fast as we were a few years ago, but we're still putting one foot in front of the other, and we're still moving in the right direction.

When we see ministry like a relay race where one generation runs and then passes the baton to the next, the question no one wants to answer is, "What does the old leader do after he passes the baton to the young leader?"

In an Olympic relay race, as soon as the baton is passed to the next runner, the previous runner is finished. He now must leave the track and find his place on the sidelines. He's no longer in the race. He has done his part. Now he watches and cheers. Maybe he does a little coaching, but he's finished running and competing. Most of my peers are not even almost ready for that. We still have races to run and finish lines to cross. So what do we do—pass the baton or hold on to the baton?

I'm now in my mid-fifties and several of my mentors are over eighty. To some of them, I will forever be that "young leader" in the Philippines. The truth is, many older leaders stubbornly refuse to pass the baton to the next generation because they don't want to leave the track and be relegated to simply watching and cheering as others run. They see themselves like Caleb—still strong and still ready to take some land. Some of these leaders plan to carry the leadership baton to the grave while strong, qualified, and frustrated younger leaders patiently and respectfully wait for the funeral where, perhaps, they'll be able to pry the baton from the hands of their spiritual fathers while no one is looking.

Russ eventually convinced most of the old guys on our North American team that there had to be a better way than keeping a death grip on the baton until we drop it, until we drop dead, or until the young leaders pry it from our cold, dead hands. Through rigorous discussions and debates, we discovered a third option. We decided that rather than keeping the baton or passing it to the next generation and watching from the stands as they run, we should create more lanes and more batons so multiple generations could continue to run toward the finish line together.

Why wrestle over one baton when there are so many great young leaders and so many amazing ministry opportunities? We decided that the better way is to not only lead the next generation, but to lead *with* the next generation. Multi-generational leadership requires us to find more batons and create more running lanes so multiple generations can run and lead together. It seems to be working for us. Most of our old leaders continue to faithfully run toward their finish line, baton in hand, while the next generation also runs with a real baton in their hands in an adjacent lane toward the same finish line. Many of us are watching next-generation leaders start to pass us. They're faster and stronger and have more endurance. Their theological depth, mission strategies, and communication skills often make ours look like a first-generation black-and-white TV, compared to giant high-definition flat screens.

I've certainly not done everything right in terms of leadership but, looking back, I have very few regrets about entrusting next-generation leaders with huge leadership responsibility. Every time I've created a new baton, then handed the previous baton to the next leader, they've finished better than I would have. Here's a brief summary of what has happened every time I created new lanes and new batons.

CREATING NEW BATONS
AND NEW LEADERSHIP LANES

After Deborah and I had served as senior pastors for six years in the original Victory U-Belt, the church had grown from zero to 600. We created another baton and another lane called Victory Makati in 1986, and in 1990, we passed the U-Belt baton to Luther Mancao and focused our time and energy on Makati. In two years, under Luther's leadership, Victory U-Belt doubled from 600 to 1,200. What took my team six years to accomplish, Luther and his team did in two.

Victory Makati started with two dozen students from Victory U-Belt who lived in the Makati area, and it took six years for that congregation to reach 700 in attendance. When we created a new baton and a new lane called Victory Shangri-la, Joey Bonifacio took the Victory Makati baton and grew the church to over 2,000 in the time it took us to grow to 700.

Victory Shangri-la eventually moved from the Shangri-la mall to Valle Verde Country Club, then to the Robinsons Galleria mall on Ortigas Avenue, and is now known as Victory Ortigas. After leading that nomadic congregation for six years, I transitioned the leadership to Ferdie Cabiling, who recently gave it to Rico Ricafort.

Under my administration, Victory Ortigas grew to about 2,000. When Ferdie gave the leadership baton to Rico Ricafort, the congregation had grown to over 7,000. Under Rico's leadership, I'm confident that our Ortigas congregation will continue to grow in depth, strength, and size. Here's the point: every time I empowered the next generation, the church grew bigger and better.

If we want to find new leadership diamonds, we'll have to look in the dirt. Once we find what vaguely resembles a potential leadership diamond, we'll then have to get our hands dirty cleaning, removing dirt, polishing, cutting, and setting.

If we want to launch new leaders, we'll have to entrust leadership responsibility to people who might not currently look like leaders. Barnabas trusted Paul. Paul trusted Timothy. We trusted Skek. Who will you trust with a significant leadership task?

Rather than passing the leadership baton and retiring or keeping the leadership baton until we die, a third option is to create new batons and new leadership lanes so several leadership generations can run the race together.

If we treat next-generation leaders like subordinates, then we will not have strong, healthy successors. But if we treat next-generation leaders like coworkers and family, then the transition to the next generation will probably be an upgrade.

DISCUSSION QUESTIONS

1. Do you include or exclude potential next-generation leaders from significant leadership situations? How can you include them more?
2. What would potentially go right or wrong if you trust young and inexperienced leaders with great leadership responsibility?
3. How can you create more lanes and more batons for young leaders?

12

HOMEGROWN OR HIRED?

Sometimes the wheel turns slowly, but it turns.
LORNE MICHAELS, TV Producer

No institution can possibly survive if it needs geniuses or supermen to manage it. It must be organized in such a way as to be able to get along under a leadership composed of average human beings.
PETER DRUCKER, Leadership Guru

I have no greater joy than to hear that my children are walking in the truth.
3 JOHN 1:4

I recently realized that at some point in my life—and I'm not exactly sure when—a major shift happened in the way I approach ministry, leadership, and maybe even life in general.

For many years, I was obsessed with trying to learn to *be* a good leader. Since I'm a natural follower, not a natural leader, I knew I had to somehow obtain basic leadership skills in order to do my job. So, I read leadership books. I took seminary classes. I studied church, political, and business leaders. I sought mentors. All of this helped (I think). But it seems like I still learned my most important leadership lessons the hard way—by taking risks, falling flat on my face, then getting up and trying again.

As time went on, leadership books, seminars, and conferences started to bore me. I was no longer internally driven to be a better leader. I am not sure whether that is good or bad, but it's the truth.

I got bored with Kouzes and Posner, Noel Tichy, Jim Collins, Robert Clinton, Aubry Malphurs, Patrick Lencioni, Hans Finzel, John Maxwell, and all the other leadership gurus and their books. But don't misunderstand me. All those men wrote great books that helped me immensely. I just couldn't read another paragraph about leadership.

I don't know when or why it happened, but I became more obsessed with how to *help those around me* become better leaders, not how to *be* a better leader myself.

Once this happened, it didn't take long for me to realize that in order to *help others become better leaders*, I would sometimes have to *get out of the way* so they could actually lead—so they could take a risk, fall flat on their faces, start over and try again, and again, and again. Just like I had done.

I NEVER RECRUITED EXTRAORDINARY LEADERS

In order to become better leaders, people need the freedom to succeed and fail without interference or intervention. As helpful as leadership books and seminary classes can be, the most lasting leadership lessons are often learned through real-life experience.

In the mid-2000s (after living in the Philippines for two decades), in an attempt to get out of the way, Deborah and I started dividing our time evenly between Nashville and Manila. We flew back and forth approximately every three months. A few years later, we gradually started scheduling more and more time away from Manila, intentionally staying out of the way for longer periods so our local leadership team could lead without worrying about my shadow. The last two years, we have started spending a bit more time in Manila again, focusing primarily on the development of younger leaders and writing new leadership material.

I realized that if I wanted to multiply leaders successfully, getting out of the way was only the beginning. Somehow, I realized that I would also have to work hard to clarify and simplify our organization. Rather than appoint a super-leader wearing stretchy pants and a cape to take our organization to the next level, I chose to work on building a healthy culture, flexible structures, and simple systems. The goal was to build an organization that was not dependent on one charismatic leader. We needed to build in such a way that a team of ordinary people and reluctant leaders would surprise themselves by leading well and over-achieving.

Jesus preferred working with ordinary people rather than superstars. In time, most of His original, non-descript disciples became spiritual superstars, but they usually didn't even realize it (and they certainly didn't care). Others noticed their extraordinary leadership and commented on it. "Now when they saw the boldness of Peter and John, and perceived that they were uneducated, common men, they were astonished. And they recognized that they had been with Jesus" (Acts 4:13).

Being with Jesus tends to make up for missing charisma and subpar education in leaders. I'm not saying that charisma and education are not helpful, just that they are not primary.

I love the way leadership guru Peter Drucker said it: "No institution can possibly survive if it needs geniuses or supermen to manage it. It must be organized in such a way as to be able to get along under a leadership composed of average human beings."

In other words, if we build our organization right, we don't need to recruit and hire "level five" super-leaders; we only need average humans. That's good news because there are a lot more average humans than super-leaders.

Because we worked hard to build a simple organization and got out of the way so ordinary humans (like us) could lead, our Filipino leaders, our Manila church, and our Delta Airlines mileage account have all grown exponentially.

For many years, I had the honor of leading a great Filipino leadership team. Now I have the honor of *leading with* a great Filipino leadership team. That's what happens when we develop homegrown ordinary leaders rather than hiring pre-made super-leaders.

"IF YOU CAN HIRE 'EM, YOU CAN HAVE 'EM"

Twice in the past fifteen years, the leaders of huge megachurches have asked me if they could hire a Victory pastor. Like many rapidly growing churches, including Victory, these two churches were experiencing an urgent leadership shortage.

The first request came from the senior pastor of a large church in a Philippine city that will remain unnamed. The pastor and I were both guest speakers at a conference.

Several Victory pastors were with me at the conference (one of them was also a guest speaker). During lunch on the second day of the conference, this megachurch pastor told me about his church's rapid growth and their never-ending leadership needs. He then spent considerable time talking about how impressed he was with Victory's leaders. Next, he started asking questions about where we found so many strong leaders. Finally, he said, "Since Victory has so many great preachers and leaders, would you mind if I hired one or two to help me?"

At first I laughed, thinking he was joking. When I realized he was serious, I said, "No problem. Do you have anyone in mind that you want to hire?"

He mentioned a couple of our pastors by name. The two he mentioned were men I had baptized, discipled, mentored, and ordained. I had officiated their weddings, dedicated their babies, and buried their parents. These men were not just staff members; they were sons, brothers, friends, family.

"Sure, feel free to interview any Victory pastor you want. As far as I'm concerned, if you can hire them, then you can have them." I paused for a few seconds, then continued, "Let me know if anyone takes your job offer, and good luck."

Even if they were offered a financial package fit for a Wall Street executive, I believed these men would never leave. Furthermore, if they were tempted to take the money and run, their wives, kids, and friends would stop them, so there was little risk in allowing this megachurch pastor from another city to recruit from my team.

I don't know if he ever interviewed any of our pastors. If he did, they declined his offer. I haven't heard from him since.

I wasn't offended by the pastor who tried to hire men I had spent years developing into leaders. In fact, it encouraged me to know that others see greatness in my team. I would hate to have a staff member that no one else would want to hire.

Another reason I wasn't bothered is because I know that sons can't be bought. They have to be birthed. And if, by chance, I happen to have a "hireling" on my staff masquerading as a son, then it would be better for all of us if he takes a higher financial offer and leaves. Whoever hires him would actually be doing us a favor.

A few years later, I received a similar second request. A pastor of an international megachurch called to inform me that they were starting a branch congregation in Manila. I was surprised they even knew we existed. When I asked how they heard of us, the pastor said that several Victory families who had migrated to their nation had joined their church. I had never heard of the Filipinos he mentioned, but they seemed to have represented Victory, the Philippines, and Jesus well.

After the pastor called me and introduced himself, he asked some great questions about cross-cultural church planting. I gave him my best answers and welcomed his church to my adopted city.

They were almost two years away from starting their Manila branch. They wisely scheduled a couple of scouting trips to meet local pastors, study the city, and pray on-site for their new church. During their first trip to Manila, a couple of Victory pastors volunteered to show them around Metro Manila and help them find the best location for their church. Since we believe that Manila doesn't have nearly enough churches, we are always glad when anyone wants to plant a new church in our city, and we are glad to do what we can to help.

About a month later, I received a call from that pastor, asking if he could hire one of the Victory pastors who had hosted his team in Manila. Again, I thought this was a joking way to express appreciation for our team's service. It took me a moment to realize that this guy, too, was serious. He said they needed a Filipino pastor for their Manila branch, and they wanted to hire one from Victory.

I answered, "Sure, you can interview any Victory pastor you want. Let me know how it works out."

Again, I really didn't mind him trying to pirate our pastors. I was confident that none of them had any interest in leaving our team, even if they would be paid in foreign currency. And, I still believed that if we had a pastor on staff who would leave us simply because of a more lucrative offer from another church, then he could go as soon as possible. Since our pastors are not here simply for a paycheck, we work with people who won't sell themselves to the highest bidder.

After I gave him my permission to interview a Victory pastor, I had to ask, "Certainly in a church with over 20,000 members . . . wait, you guys do have more than 20,000, right?" He confirmed this to be true. I continued, "In a church that big, you should have at least two dozen leaders you can send to Manila. Why not promote from within?"

He said they had no leaders and asked again if it would be okay if he interviewed a Victory pastor for the job.

They ended up hiring a pastor from one of Manila's other churches. I am sure he will do a great job for them, and I sincerely hope that their church does well and reaches tens of thousands of Filipinos with the gospel.

We've had seasons in Victory with serious leadership shortages. During those times though, we never looked outside to solve our leadership problem. We never put a "Help Wanted" ad on a seminary bulletin board or in a Christian magazine.

Even during our most severe leadership droughts, we have always assumed that our future leaders were right in front of us, hiding in plain sight, waiting for us to identify and instruct them. A little impartation and an internship would also help, but we know they are already in our church, waiting for an opportunity to minister and lead. Like diamonds in the rough, as Skek said, many times our future leaders are buried in the dirt. Leadership shortages are a clarion call for us to get our hands dirty—to dig for leaders who will sparkle like diamonds as soon as we clean, cut, polish, and set them.

I believe that our church has all the potential leaders we need, and I believe that your church has all the potential leaders you need. The question is, if our potential leaders are there, how do we find and develop them? And how do we make sure we don't spend our time and energy developing "hirelings" who will leave us as soon as the grass looks greener on the other side?

SHOW ME THE MONEY

Jesus told a parable about people who are hired hands or "hirelings" (KJV), contrasting them with the "good shepherd."

> "I am the good shepherd. The good shepherd lays down his life for the sheep. He who is a *hired hand* and not a shepherd, who does not own the sheep, sees the wolf

coming and leaves the sheep and flees, and the wolf snatches them and scatters them. He flees because he is a *hired hand* and cares nothing for the sheep. I am the good shepherd. I know my own and my own know me, just as the Father knows me and I know the Father; and I lay down my life for the sheep." (John 10:11–15)

According to Jesus, the good shepherd actually knows the sheep, cares about their wellbeing, and is willing to sacrifice his life for them. The hired hand is the exact opposite. He doesn't really know the sheep, does not care about them, and runs away at the first hint of discomfort or danger.

When we hire leaders from other ministries, luring them with bigger salaries and better titles, we usually get what we pay for—hired hands who will run away as soon as tough times happen or better opportunities present themselves. When we grow our own from the ground up, because they have been with us for many years, they actually know and care about the people. Because of long-term relationships, homegrown leaders are rarely looking for greener grass.

In summary, hirelings are driven by their relationship with money and are willing to sacrifice anything to get more. Good shepherds are driven by their relationship with the sheep, willing to sacrifice even their lives to protect the sheep.

At this point, I feel the need to write a quick disclaimer, lest anyone misunderstand me. I am not saying that salaries are unimportant or unspiritual. The Apostle Paul certainly believed in paying pastors decent salaries. Notice what he wrote to Timothy about local church leadership. "Let the elders who rule well be considered worthy of double honor, especially those who labor in preaching and teaching. For the Scripture says, 'You shall not muzzle an ox when it treads out the grain,' and, 'The laborer deserves his wages'" (1 Timothy 5:17–18). The "muzzle an ox" metaphor is an obvious reference to paying the pastor or elder.

Similarly, Paul quotes the same verse from Deuteronomy when writing about money to the Corinthian church.

> For it is written in the Law of Moses, "You shall not muzzle an ox when it treads out the grain." Is it for oxen that God is concerned? Does he not certainly speak for our sake? It was written for our sake, because the plowman should plow in hope and the thresher thresh in hope of sharing in the crop. If we have sown spiritual things among you, is it too much if we reap material things from you? (1 Corinthians 9:9–11)

Again, this whole Corinthian discourse is about money and generosity, so I am not suggesting that anyone with a salary is a hireling.

Money is necessary in this world. It is a tool for ministry. It is a blessing from God. But it can sometimes be a temptation or trap.

Pastors should be honored, and they should be paid. If you are a pastor, I hope you are doubly honored and well paid. I also hope God delivers you from staff and leaders who are hirelings; people who are only in it for the money, people who only see ministry as a job.

Clearly, we don't want hired hands; we want homegrown leaders who actually care.

Perhaps looking at another industry might shed some light on the strategy for leadership discovery.

HOMEGROWN COMEDIANS

As you read the following list of famous comedians and big-time movie stars, see if you can guess what they all have in common:

Will Ferrell	Eddie Murphy	Jim Belushi
Jimmy Fallon	Chevy Chase	Dan Aykroyd
Chris Rock	Mike Myers	David Spade
Adam Sandler	Chris Farley	Dana Carvey
Tina Fey	Bill Murray	Phil Hartman
Amy Poehler	John Belushi	

This list includes some of the most famous and highest-paid comedians and comedy actors in the world. They have individually earned millions of dollars. Their films have collectively earned billions of dollars.

But what do they all have in common?

Every person on the list is a homegrown talent of a Canadian television producer, writer, and comedic genius named Lorne Michaels. Everyone on the list became famous because of an American television variety show Michaels created called *Saturday Night Live,* or simply *SNL.* The multi-awarded show is now in its forty-first season.

After the surprise meteoric success of the first few seasons, Michaels' previously unknown comedians were constantly being lured away from *SNL* by lucrative movie offers.

Year after year, as soon as *SNL* would lose a talent like Chevy Chase, the next season, Michaels would discover an Eddie Murphy. One season, Michaels lost Mike Myers, Chris Farley, and Adam Sandler, but the next season, he discovered Jimmy Fallon, Will Ferrell, and Tina Fey. This process repeated itself for over forty seasons, with a couple of exceptions.

In 1984, after losing some more newly famous *SNL* comedians to the film industry, the producers decided to break with their successful pattern of turning homegrown nobodies into global superstars, and for the first time, they hired established comedians to fill their cast. They did the same thing in 1985. The established talent they recruited included Billy Crystal, Martin Short, Robert Downey Jr., Joan Cusack, and Dennis Miller.

What was the result of hiring established, famous, high-salaried comedians rather than taking the risk with homegrown unknowns? Well, while the 1984 season was successful, the show was almost cancelled after a lackluster 1985 season.

In 1986, they returned to their winning formula, firing the famous high-priced veterans and replacing them with homegrown nobodies, including Dana Carvey and Phil Hartman. The show was back on track and has continued to discover and take a risk with previous unknowns who have eventually become global superstars.

If you're a pastor or campus missionary, please note that *SNL* got off-track when they decided to import famous talent from the outside rather than growing unknown talent from within. The mistake was to hire successful stars, rather than take the risk with inexperienced potential. Again, I believe that every future leader you need is right in front of you, hiding like Gideon, waiting for you to call them into greatness. (See Judges 6 for the story of Gideon, the insecure and reluctant leader.)

If Lorne Michaels can consistently transform relatively unknown and inexperienced upstart comedians into global comedy giants, then I believe that every church or campus-ministry leader reading this book can also see young, inexperienced, average humans transformed into God-honoring, disciple-making, world-changing global leaders.

SOME LEADERS ARE ADOPTED

Before we talk about how to discover and develop home-grown leaders, I need to say that it is possible to have a homegrown leader who was "grafted in" or adopted.

I have many friends who have adopted children. Some families adopted kids of the same ethnicity as the parents, and if they didn't tell you which kid was adopted, you would never be able to guess. I also know families who have adopted kids of different ethnicities. It's visually obvious which kids were adopted, yet they are equally loved and accepted. The adopted kids also have the same responsibilities and inheritance as the biological kids. That's how it is in the church family.

Most Victory pastors and leaders are homegrown, meaning they got saved, baptized, discipled, married, equipped, empowered, trained, and ordained in Victory. A small number of Victory leaders are also homegrown, but they were saved, baptized, married, trained, ordained, hired, and sometimes fired by other ministries. Through the providence of God, they landed at Victory and got encouraged, connected, equipped, empowered, retrained, re-ordained, and now serve on our team. I am thankful for both the leaders who were born in Victory and for those who were adopted.

My good friend, Luther Mancao, was saved, baptized, trained, and ordained in a Southern Baptist church. His church, Praise Fellowship, was our next-door neighbor in the University Belt. Victory and Praise did worship, prayer, and campus outreach together. It was obvious to his team and ours that God was connecting our churches.

When we officially merged in 1990, you know from the previous chapter that I made Luther the senior pastor of the University Belt congregation, and I concentrated on our new Makati congregation. We not only got Luther and Nanette in the deal, we also got his amazing team that included Rouel Asuncion, who leads Every Nation Dubai, Ed Ty who leads Victory Lucena, and Robert Hern who now leads Victory San Diego. Luther, Rouel, Ed, and Robert are as "Victory" as anyone who got saved and discipled during our original outreach in 1984.

So, where do homegrown leaders come from, and how do we develop them?

HOW TO GROW YOUR OWN

Genesis 14 records the story of King Chedorlaomer and his allies fighting against the kings of Sodom and Gomorrah and their allies. Abraham's nephew, Lot, who was foolishly living in Sodom at the time, was captured during the conflict. An unnamed person escaped captivity and told Abraham about the plight of Lot and his family. Notice Abraham's response.

"When Abram heard that his kinsman had been taken captive, he led forth his trained men, *born in his house*, 318 of them, and went in pursuit as far as Dan" (Genesis 14:14).

Without getting bogged down in the details of the story, I'll summarize it by saying that Abraham and his 318 homegrown leaders risked their lives to rescue Lot's family.

This simple verse gives us three characteristics that describe Abraham's homegrown leaders.

1. They were "born in his house."
2. They were "trained men."
3. They were willing to be "led forth" into a dangerous battle.

So, what can we learn from this story about developing homegrown leaders?

- **Birth them.** Abraham started with men "born in his house." We start by reaching the lost with the gospel, rather than trying to attract members from the church down the road. The best homegrown leaders are usually those born in our house. Yes, some are adopted, but most are birthed. So, the more we preach the gospel to lost people, the more homegrown leaders we will have.

- **Train them.** Abraham had "trained men" ready when disaster struck. We need to start training and equipping our people as soon as their hair dries after water baptism. Don't wait for maturity. Train them now. It doesn't matter if you don't have a great world-class training school. Start on-the-job training right now. The more you train, the better your training track will become. Any training is better than none.

- **Lead them.** Abraham's 318 men were willing to be "led forth" even if it required sacrifice. And Abraham was not hesitant to lead them. The best potential leaders are people who are willing to follow leadership. If we birth them and train them but don't lead them, we will not have strong leaders. They need your leadership and direction.

This birth, train, and lead principle not only works if you need an army to rescue a wayward relative, but it is also effective in developing homegrown pastors, campus missionaries, and comedy actors.

LEADERSHIP IS RELATIONSHIP

When I think about "homegrown leaders," I obviously think of two words: *home* and *grown*. Home is where family lives; grown or growth implies progress. From start to finish, this book has addressed the idea of growing. Let's take a minute and think about the "home" part of home-grown. Home is simply where family lives, and family is all about relationship.

For Jesus, leadership development was not a formal class to teach or an impersonal program to run. Like everything else He did, leadership was rooted in relationship. When Jesus related to people, it was not a surface, casual relationship, but a deep, sacrificial relationship. His relationships were the closest relationships imaginable—like family.

Notice that when Jesus was informed that that His mother and brothers were looking for Him, He used that encounter to teach an important truth about discipleship and leadership. He replied to the man, "'Who is my mother, and who are my brothers?' And stretching out his hand toward his disciples, he said, 'Here are my mother and my brothers! For whoever does the will of my Father in heaven is my brother and sister and mother'" (Matthew 12:48–50).

Jesus was not implying that our discipleship and leadership relationships should replace family relationships. Rather, He was teaching that discipleship, like family, should be relational.

Jesus was not the only person in the Bible to use family words to describe discipleship and leadership. Here are a few other examples.

- **Paul.** In his letters to his friends in Thessalonica, Paul did not use hierarchical ecclesiastical titles. Rather, he used family terms to identify himself. In several verses, he referred to himself as a *brother.* Then he reminded them that he dealt with them as a *"father* deals with his own children."* He even said that he and his team were "gentle among you like a *mother* caring for her little children" (1 Thessalonians 2:7,9,11, NIV). Rather than reminding the Thessalonians of his apostolic position and authority, Paul reminded them that he treated them like a brother, father, and mother. Like Jesus, Paul saw discipleship and leadership development as deeply relational, not primarily organizational.

- **James.** Even though he really was the brother of Jesus (they had the same mother), James seemed to call just about everyone his *brother.* In his epistle, James wrote to brothers who were going through trials, brothers who were in humble circumstances, brothers who talked too much, brothers who showed favoritism, brothers who had faith without works, brothers who wanted to be teachers, brothers with untamed tongues, brothers who slandered, brothers who were impatient, brothers who grumbled, brothers who swore, and brothers who wandered away. To James, discipleship was like a living room filled with brothers, not a classroom filled with students.

- **Peter.** Even a tough, aggressive, and seemingly non-relational leader like Peter described discipleship and leadership with relational family words. He referred to Silas as his faithful *brother*. He called Mark his *son*.

- **John.** Like James and Peter, John often used the word *brother* to describe the men he discipled and led. He famously wrote that he had "no greater joy than to hear that my *children* are walking in the truth" (3 John 1:4). These children he wrote about were not his flesh-and-blood sons and daughters, but spiritual sons and daughters. Unfortunately today in the church, even the family terms of endearment like "father" and "brother" have often become dead religious titles. Real leadership, patterned after the New Testament, will function like a family. This does not mean we must call each other "brother" and "sister," but we must treat each other like brothers and sisters.

LEADERSHIP AND THE JADE CABBAGE

A few years ago, our Every Nation Asia Leadership Team (ALT) held its annual strategic planning meeting in Taipei, Taiwan. The ALT includes Every Nation leaders from China, Malaysia, Singapore, the Philippines, and other nations in the region. After three full days of productive ministry work, we planned a day to be tourists.

As tourists, we were all surprised by a profound leadership lesson from the famous Jade Cabbage. No, the Jade Cabbage is not a character from a *Kung Fu Panda* movie. It is the most famous piece of carved jade in the history of jade carving.

Here's how our unforgettable Jade Cabbage encounter came to be. We were told that if we wanted to see the architecture of ancient China, we should visit the Forbidden City in mainland China. But if we wanted to see the art and treasures of ancient China, we should visit the National Palace Museum in Taipei. Since we were in Taipei, we chose the art and treasure tour. Oddly enough, the National Palace Museum in Taipei is the national museum of the Republic of China (mainland China). It houses over 650,000 pieces of ancient Chinese art and artifacts covering over 8,000 years of Chinese history—an amazing museum experience!

We were surprised and somewhat puzzled to discover that the most revered artifact in the whole museum is the famous Jade Cabbage. A close second is the equally famous Jade Pork. The Chinese do love their food.

Compared to all the amazing artifacts, I could not understand the fascination with a piece of jade carved to look like a cabbage. I had to ask. Here's the story from the museum guide, who is one of the world's foremost experts on jade carvings.

The chunk of jade chosen by the artist was a second-class grade of jade with many visible imperfections. Despite the numerous flaws, the artist saw the potential and started carving what would become a famous and priceless stone vegetable. I'm still not sure why hundreds of people line up every day to view the Jade Cabbage, but an important leadership lesson was reinforced as the museum guide proudly shared his knowledge of carved jade.

Here's that lesson: even if we are working with people who have visible flaws, healthy leadership development always focuses on the potential, not on the problem. The four leadership multipliers—identification, instruction, impartation, and internship—help carve away the imperfections so the human version of the Jade Cabbage can emerge, for the honor of God and the good of humanity.

The best leaders are homegrown. While most homegrown leaders will be "born in [the] house," some will be adopted.

You already have all the potential leaders you need, you just need to identify and develop them.

Once we identify potential leaders who are already with us, rather than hiring veteran leaders from the outside, we can apply the principles of instruction, impartation, and internship. The end result of our leadership-development strategy will be homegrown leaders.

DISCUSSION QUESTIONS X

1. Can you list at least three people whom you are planning to develop as leaders? What is your next step for each?
2. Who helped develop you as a leader? How did they help you?
3. Do you view leadership as deeply relational? Are you developing strong roots with the men or women you're leading?

13

PLATFORMS OR PRISONS?

We are like dwarves perched on the shoulders of giants, and thus we are able to see more and farther than the latter. And this is not at all because of the acuteness of our sight or the stature of our body, but because we are carried aloft and elevated by the magnitude of the giants.

BERNARD OF CHARTRES, Philosopher

The ultimate test of a person's leadership is the health of the organization when the organizer is gone.

J. OSWALD SANDERS, Missiologist

Now Absalom in his lifetime had taken and set up for himself the pillar that is in the King's Valley, for he said, "I have no son to keep my name in remembrance." He called the pillar after his own name, and it is called Absalom's monument to this day.

2 SAMUEL 18:18

In 2009, Deborah and I went to Israel for a ten-day study tour for pastors. On the eighth day, we were in Jerusalem's Kidron Valley, standing at the base of a twenty-meter (or sixty-five foot) tall monument. My brain was saturated with information, revelation, and application. I had furiously taken notes for the first seven days. But since my notebook was as full as my brain, I had given up and closed the notebook the day before. Now I was simply listening in a zombie-like state. Then I heard a story that snapped me back to attention. This became one of the most unforgettable leadership lessons of the entire trip. Our tour guide, Arie Bar-David, said:

> Tradition tells us that for hundreds of years, Jews and Christians and Muslims who lived in Jerusalem would bring their disobedient children to this very spot to throw stones at *Yad Avshalom* (Absalom's monument) as a reminder of the fate of those who rebel against their fathers.

Standing in the shadow of this massive monument, pen and notebook in hand, I was now writing down another poignant leadership lesson from our master Bible teacher and tour guide extraordinaire. As with all of Arie's stories, we were hanging on every word, and at the same time, trying to discern every word despite his thick Israeli accent.

The biblical account of Absalom's leadership arrogance had always fascinated and terrified me, so I forced myself to listen and learn. And I silently prayed that God would deliver me from the character flaws that led to Absalom's leadership crash.

My youngest son Jonathan, who was nineteen years old at the time, accompanied us on the tour. One of my favorite photos from that trip features Jonathan and I looking like tiny ants while standing shoulder-to-shoulder on the cube-shaped foundation, dwarfed by Absalom's massive stone tower. Every time I look at that photo, it silently warns me of the subtle but destructive power of leadership arrogance, and it reminds me that the world doesn't need a monument with my name on it.

According to Arie, this giant monument to an arrogant leader was carved into the side of the Mount of Olives about 3,000 years ago. Some modern scholars have recently claimed that it was actually constructed around AD 100. Either way, it has traditionally been known as Absalom's monument for quite a long time, and for hundreds of years, parents and children have tossed stones at it. Whether this tradition is based on legend or fact, the lessons the monument teaches are important truths that all leaders should take to heart.

Here's what the Bible says about Absalom's monument:

Now Absalom in his lifetime had taken and set up for himself the pillar that is in the King's Valley, for he said, "I have no son to keep my name in remembrance." He called the pillar after his own name, and it is called Absalom's monument to this day. (2 Samuel 18:18)

WHY LEADERS BUILD MONUMENTS TO THEMSELVES

Who was Absalom, and why did he build a massive monument to himself? Here's my quick answer to that complicated question. The third son of King David and the daughter of Maacah, Absalom was the most handsome man in the kingdom (2 Samuel 14:25), kind of like an ancient Mr. Universe or Derek Zoolander, who was "really, really ridiculously good-looking." Absalom had a sister named Tamar who would play an important role in his tragic story.

He had three sons and one daughter. His daughter was also named Tamar, after her aunt (2 Samuel 14:27). Remember that name, Tamar. We will get to the significance of her part in the story soon enough.

There are many reasons leaders build monuments to honor themselves. Here are the top three reasons from the sad story of Absalom.

1. Leaders who refuse to honor their fathers build monuments to themselves. Toward the end of David's rule, Absalom secretly and strategically "stole the hearts of the people of Israel" by dishonoring and undermining his father. (See 2 Samuel 15:1–6.) Instead of going to war against his rebellious son, King David and his officials decided to flee from Jerusalem, allowing Absalom to set up his renegade kingdom in the palace.

What kind of leader builds a monument to himself? The kind of leader who dishonors, disrespects, and undermines his father. Leaders will either honor their fathers or they will honor themselves. They can't do both.

David honored King Saul even though Saul was difficult to honor for many reasons. Solomon later honored King David, even though David had several humiliating public failures. But Absalom chose to honor himself and therefore, dishonored his father, King David.

This brief history of Absalom explains why, when parents are looking for a Bible name for their firstborn son, the name Absalom doesn't even make the Top 500 list. Absalom is in the bottom five, along with Ahab, Doeg, Herod, and Judas.

Refusing to honor his father was bad enough, but that was only the first step that made Absalom the poster boy for arrogant leadership. The next step was his refusal to forgive his brother.

2. Leaders who refuse to forgive their brothers build monuments to themselves. Absalom had an evil half-brother named Amnon, who was one of King David's many sons. Amnon had an unnatural attraction to his beautiful half-sister, Tamar. Burning with lust, Amnon and a friend devised a plot to lure Tamar into his room. He pretended to be sick, and as expected, Tamar responded with compassion, made some food, and delivered it to his room.

Here's the biblical narrative.

> . . . Tamar took the cakes she had made and brought them into the chamber to Amnon her brother. But when she brought them near him to eat, he took hold of her and said to her, "Come, lie with me, my sister." She answered him, "No, my brother, do not violate me, for such a thing is not done in Israel; do not do this outrageous thing. As for me, where could I carry my shame? And as for you, you would be as one of the outrageous fools in Israel." . . . But he would not listen to her, and being stronger than she, he violated her and lay with her. (2 Samuel 13:10–14)

After being raped by her half-brother, Tamar took refuge in Absalom's house. The Bible tells us that while he said nothing negative to or about Amnon, nevertheless, "Absalom hated Amnon, because he had violated his sister" (2 Samuel 13:21).

For two whole years, Absalom nursed his hatred until it turned to bitterness and took deep root in his heart. The book of Hebrews teaches that a "bitter root" will grow up to cause trouble and will eventually defile many (Hebrews 12:15, NIV). Trouble and defilement is an understatement in the case of Absalom and Amnon.

About the time that everyone thought the ugly instance was behind them, Absalom invited all of his brothers and half-brothers, including Amnon, to a big sheepshearer convention near Ephraim. With King David's approval, everyone attended. And when they least expected it, the bitter root in Absalom sprang up and bore its violent fruit.

> Then Absalom commanded his servants, "Mark when Amnon's heart is merry with wine, and when I say to you, 'Strike Amnon,' then kill him. Do not fear; have I not commanded you? Be courageous and be valiant." So the servants of Absalom did to Amnon as Absalom had commanded. . . . (2 Samuel 13:28–29)

The question is, what type of leader builds a monument to himself? The answer is threefold. First, leaders who refuse to honor their fathers build monuments to themselves. Second, leaders who refuse to forgive their brothers build monuments to themselves. And third . . .

3. Leaders who refuse to trust their sons build monuments to themselves. The original verse that mentions Absalom's monument gives more insight into why he built the massive monument to himself: "for he said, 'I have no son to keep my name in remembrance.'" So he built it and named it after himself because he had no son to carry his name.

Wait a minute. The Bible says, "There were born to Absalom *three sons*, and one daughter whose name was Tamar. She was a beautiful woman" (2 Samuel 14:27). If the Bible says he had three sons, why did Absalom think he had no son to carry his name? Some interpreters have speculated that perhaps all three of his sons died. This is unlikely, as deaths of the sons of kings were usually mentioned and the Bible doesn't mention these heirs to the throne dying prematurely.

Absalom had three sons, but the Bible records that "he said, 'I have no son to keep my name in remembrance.'" Perhaps he felt this way because he had dishonored his father's good name, and he assumed that his sons would follow his example and dishonor him. So, "he called the pillar after his own name."

Whatever the inner motivation, Absalom, like many leaders before and after him, built a massive monument to himself.

MODERN MONUMENTS TO INSECURE LEADERS

Absalom was neither the first nor the last self-absorbed arrogant leader to build a monument for his own honor. Two generations before Absalom's monument was built, King Saul—the man whom Absalom's father honored and forgave—built his own monument. Samuel writes that "'Saul came to Carmel, and behold, he set up a monument for himself . . .'" (1 Samuel 15:12). Even though Saul had all the external traits that might make one a great leader, inside he was painfully insecure. His insecurity only increased as he wrestled with the possibility that David, rather than his beloved son Jonathan, would one day succeed him on the throne. Of course, Jonathan had no problem with his best friend David succeeding his father. But that did not stop insecure King Saul from trying to kill David on multiple occasions.

How often do insecurity and self-preservation cause leaders who are nearing the end of their race to resist crowning their obvious successor?

If Absalom built a monument to his arrogance, then Saul built a monument to his insecurity. This combination of insecurity and arrogance is a lethal mix when one is in a position of leadership. Unless both are dealt with deep in the leader's heart, a fall is just around the corner.

Insecure and arrogant leaders still build monuments to themselves today. They're not usually called monuments, and they rarely carry the leader's name, but nevertheless, they're monuments to insecure men.

A couple of decades ago, while visiting relatives and mission partners in Atlanta, Deborah and I had a rare Sunday off, so we visited a famous mega-church that was one of the largest churches in America at the time. Sadly, that church no longer exists. After a series of pastoral moral failures and cover-ups (plus some questionable theology), the church growth gradually plateaued, then started shrinking, and eventually, the church simply and quietly vanished.

If I were to do an autopsy on that church, obviously the adultery, cover-up, and bad theology contributed to its demise. But looking back to the day Deborah and I visited that once-great church, I think I can point out some small cracks in the foundation that possibly led to moral and theological compromise (ultimately destroying that church). (Note: This story was borrowed from chapter 8, "The Man of God Syndrome," of my book *WikiChurch*.)

This huge multi-ethnic church seemed to have all the essentials for a successful modern megachurch: great location, huge campus, beautiful buildings, slick logo, state-of-the-art lighting and sound, and a television ministry. Of course, there's nothing necessarily wrong with a church having any or all of these things. Having stuff is never the problem. However, having a divided heart and a wrong motive is always problematic. And, as mentioned above, the insecurity and arrogance combo in leadership is a deadly mix.

It's difficult to imagine, but two decades before the advent of social media, the founding pastor of this massive, growing, and globally influential megachurch was somehow able to take ministerial self-promotion to a whole new level. In today's narcissistic, selfie-obsessed world, it's possible that some pastor has managed to surpass this guy, but in his day, he was the undisputed king of self-promotion.

During the sermon, I counted ten photos of the pastor on the four-page church bulletin. As I left the sanctuary and made my way to the parking lot, I noticed his family name on most of the buildings, including the small wedding chapel, the education building, and the youth center. It seemed like this guy was attempting to outdo Absalom, who only had one monument with his name.

Rather than encouraging or allowing celebrity hero worship in our churches, we need leaders who run from misdirected over-honor. For example, watch what happened when the crowd at Lystra tried to worship Paul and Barnabas after God healed a crippled man: "And when the crowds saw what Paul had done, they lifted up their voices, saying in Lycaonian, 'The gods have come down to us in the likeness of men!'" (Acts 14:11). The confused but zealous local priests started preparing animals to be sacrificed to Paul and Barnabas. (Read Acts 14 for the whole story.)

THE DANGER OF OVER-HONOR
What should a leader do when legitimate honor creeps toward idolatrous worship?

Insecure leaders desire a level of honor that's unhealthy, and they often intentionally create a culture of over-honor that borders on idolatry. This can make multiplying leaders difficult. Healthy leaders don't orchestrate hero-worship moments. In fact, over-honor makes healthy leaders extremely uncomfortable. But sometimes, they find themselves in these moments. So what's a leader to do? Notice how Paul and Barnabas responded when they realized they were about to have animals sacrificed to them.

> But when the apostles Barnabas and Paul heard of it, they tore their garments and rushed out into the crowd, crying out, "Men, why are you doing these things? We also are men, of like nature with you, and we bring you good news, that you should turn from these vain things to a living God, who made the heaven and the earth and the sea and all that is in them." (Acts 14:14–15)

Paul and Barnabas reminded the people and themselves that they were men, not gods. It might be good for spiritual leaders to remind themselves and one another of the reality of their humanity every now and then. After clarifying their anthropological position, Paul and Barnabas also addressed the faulty theology of the misguided Lyconians by preaching the gospel of Christ.

John the Baptist was another leader who stayed grounded in reality by successfully deflecting over-honor. As John's crowds were growing larger and larger and his followers wanted to know if he might be their long-awaited Messiah, "He confessed, and did not deny, but confessed, 'I am not the Christ'" (John 1:20).

Whoever said that confession is good for the soul was probably talking about confessing sin. But I think that confessing our humanity and reminding ourselves that we are not messiahs is also good for the soul.

Here's a suggestion for megachurch pastors who have huge churches, global influence, and adoring fans: occasionally look at the man in the mirror and confess, "I am not the Messiah."

Leaders, especially church and mission leaders, need to get over themselves, refuse to be worshiped, and realize that ministry is always about the next generation.

THE ACCOUNT OF MY LIFE

While I had worked tirelessly for my first ten years in Manila to identify, develop, and multiply next-generation Filipino leaders, the importance of that idea took a radical turn one day while sitting in an Asian Theological Seminary class taught by Dr. Nomer Bernardino. I enjoyed every lecture and discussion in Nomer's class on the book of Genesis.

Here's the gist of what I learned that day and how it drove me to live and lead for the next generation. (Note: This is also mentioned in chapter 1, "Gone With the Wind," of my book *My First, Second & Third Attempts at Parenting*.)

Our modern Bibles divide Genesis into fifty chapters. The original text didn't include chapter and verse numbers, but the writer of Genesis did include ten clearly marked sections. Some sections are long and some are shorter. Every time the phrase "This is the account of" (NIV) appears, it indicates a new topic or section. A quick look at some of these ten sections reveals God's view of multi-generational continuity.

In Genesis 11:27 we find this section marker, "This is the account of Terah." After reading that statement, one would expect to read all about Terah's life and accomplishments. But surprisingly, only six verses are directly about Terah while thirteen chapters are about Terah's son, Abraham. When the Bible recorded the account of Terah's life, it was primarily about the accomplishments of the next generation.

Likewise, in Genesis 25:19 we read, "This is the account of Abraham's son, Isaac." This time we get a mere three verses about Isaac, followed by eleven chapters about his sons, Esau and Jacob. Again, we learn that the account of a man is mostly about what the next generation does.

This pattern is repeated in Genesis 37:2. "This is the account of Jacob." This time we get only one verse about Jacob followed by fourteen chapters about his sons, primarily Joseph.

What I learned in Nomer's seminary class on the book of Genesis has made a great impact on the way I do life, leadership, and ministry, more than all my other seminary classes together.

According to the pattern in Genesis, when God records the account of a person's life, He focuses primarily on the next generation's accomplishments and failures. This tells me that when God writes the account of my life, He will include a comment or two about me, followed by multiple chapters about my sons, William, James, and Jonathan.

I'm convinced that His account of my life and ministry will also include chapter after chapter about my spiritual sons. The real and eternal account of my life will have little to do with the size of my church, how many books I sold, or how many people followed me on Twitter. From God's perspective, the primary account of my life can only be measured long after I am dead and buried, and the next-generation leaders approach their finish lines. Therefore, my leadership position is never about my personal success. It's always about preparing the next generation for success and for succession.

MULTI-GENERATIONAL FAILURE

God's perspective as presented in Genesis is multi-generational, long-term, and eternal. The typical human perspective is tragically self-absorbed, short-term, and temporal. The poster boy for short-term, single-generational leadership is King Hezekiah. Oddly enough, Hezekiah was one of the few Old Testament kings who did right before the Lord. He humbly listened and faithfully obeyed when Isaiah the prophet spoke. He served his God, his city, his nation, and his people. Yet, his son, Manasseh, was one of the most evil kings in the history of ancient Israel.

How does such a godly leader raise such an ungodly son? I'm sure the answer to that question is complicated, but at least part of the answer is by rejecting God's multi-generational vision.

Toward the end of his reign, when King Merodach from Babylon sent envoys to visit King Hezekiah at his palace, Hezekiah made a major leadership blunder that seriously violated national security protocols. Maybe he was arrogantly trying to impress the Babylonians or maybe it was simply a temporary lapse of judgment, but King Hezekiah foolishly allowed foreign spies to see everything in his palace, including his royal treasury, armory, and storehouses.

When Isaiah heard what his king had done, he immediately knew that there would be tragic national repercussions, and he knew he had to deliver a word from God to King Hezekiah. That word essentially said that Babylon would attack Jerusalem and "that which your fathers have stored up till this day, shall be carried to Babylon. Nothing shall be left, says the Lord" (2 Kings 20:17).

Being attacked and pillaged by a foreign enemy is bad, but that was not the worst consequence of Hezekiah's leadership failure. The second part of Isaiah's message was much worse than losing material belongings. "And some of your own sons, who shall be born to you, shall be taken away, and they shall be eunuchs in the palace of the king of Babylon" (2 Kings 20:18). As a father of three sons, I cannot imagine what I would do if a prophet told me that my bad leadership decision would result in the captivity of my sons. I think I would do anything in my power to stop this horrible fate from happening.

Every time I read Hezekiah's response to Isaiah's word, I get mad and I want to shout at him and at every leader who does not care what happens to the next generation.

> "Then Hezekiah said to Isaiah, 'The word of the Lord that you have spoken is good.' For he thought, 'Why not, if there will be peace and security in my days?'" (2 Kings 20:19)

Hezekiah's response is one of the saddest stories in the whole Bible. Don't forget that Hezekiah was a righteous king. Righteous leaders say and do dumb things when they reject God's multi-generational mission.

How can anyone say that Isaiah's word is good? What is good about the next generation being destroyed? That word is only good to a leader who thinks exclusively about his generation with no concern about what happens to the generations that follow. Unfortunately, many modern leaders think just like Hezekiah. They are righteous, and they only care about their own generation. As long as there is peace and prosperity in their lifetime, what comes next doesn't concern them.

In stark contrast to King Hezekiah's view of the next generation, let's go back to God's multi-generational vision for Abraham:

". . . To your offspring I will give this land. . . ." (Genesis 12:7).

". . . all the land that you see I will give to you and to your offspring forever" (Genesis 13:15).

". . . number the stars . . . So shall your offspring be" (Genesis 15:5).

"To your offspring I give this land, from the river of Egypt to the great river, the river Euphrates . . ." (Genesis 15:18).

"And I will establish my covenant between me and you and your offspring after you throughout their generations for an everlasting covenant . . ." (Genesis 17:7).

"And I will give to you and to your offspring after you the land of your sojournings . . ." (Genesis 17:8).

It's obvious from these verses that God's vision for Abraham also included the next generation. I'm sure that God's vision for Hezekiah also included the next generation, but Hezekiah missed that part. Abraham did not miss that part. He prepared the next generation for success.

ARE YOU BUILDING
A PLATFORM OR A PRISON?

Several years ago, I preached at a church in Dallas that was pastored by my friend Joe Martin. After arriving, Joe couldn't wait to show me the progress on their new building. When I say new, I mean new to Trinity Church. The church building was actually very old and in need of some serious renovation. I had seen the old building the year before and had heard the miracle provision story that had enabled Trinity to purchase the facility, so I was excited to see the new-and-improved version. As Joe toured me through the lobby, the kids' facilities, and the prayer room, I was quite impressed with the transformation. But the new sanctuary was the highlight of my tour.

"Steve, step up here with me," Joe said in his signature thick Dallas accent. As I did as I was told, Joe proudly informed me, "My dad built this platform."

Joe's dad, Joe Martin Sr., had driven from Tennessee to Dallas to help with the church renovation project. Joe explained that his dad had personally cut, nailed, and stained the hardwood boards that formed the worship platform we were standing on.

But that was not all.

"Let me show you something else." Joe was pointing to a beautiful but simple wood podium that was on center stage, as he proudly explained, "My dad cut down an oak tree from the family farm and made this pulpit from that wood. It was his surprise gift to me."

I was thoroughly impressed with Joe Martin Sr.'s woodworking skills, but what Joe said next is a leadership lesson I don't think I will ever forget. "Every Sunday, I get to stand on a platform and preach from a pulpit that my dad built."

Wow! That's what multi-generational leadership is all about—building a platform for the next generation. But sadly, many leaders follow the example of King Hezekiah and build only for their own generation.

Some leaders build prisons rather than platforms.

As I stood on the platform and admired the pulpit that Joe's dad built, I remembered a story in a book I had read several years before. The book had an odd title, *Hippo in the Garden*. It was written by a pastor named James Ryle. I don't remember anything in that book except for the title and one story. Here's that story.

By the age of six, James Ryle was in an orphanage. By the time he turned nineteen, he was in the Texas State Penitentiary. By the grace of God, he heard and responded to the gospel and became a pastor, a founding board member of Promise Keepers, a much sought-after speaker, and a best-selling author.

It's a long story, but James eventually sought and found the father he never knew. It didn't take long to discover that they had both been incarcerated. Here's an early father-son conversation as told in Ryle's book, *Released from the Prison My Father Built*.

"Dad, which prison were you in?"

"I was in the Central Unit," he replied, unaware of all that was lingering behind my question. The moment I heard his answer my countenance dropped. It was not the same prison unit I had been in. I had thought for sure it was going to be the same and had envisioned preaching rousing sermons about being in the same prison that your father was in; you know, the old "like father, like son" thing. But none of this mattered now. His answer changed all that.

"Which prison were you in?" he then asked me, not knowing how my mind was racing.

Somewhat dejected, I replied, "I was in the Ferguson Unit, near Midway, Texas; just down a ways from Huntsville."

My dad's expression changed immediately. He went from being curious, to being stunned. His mouth dropped open, and he looked at me in disbelief. Gathering himself, he then said the words that would forever mark my life.

"Dear God, son, I built that prison."

"What?" I replied, "What do you mean, you built it?"

"They used prison labor to build the Ferguson Unit," dad answered. "I was the welder on the work crew. I welded the bars when that prison was built."

Just as James Ryle was literally trapped in a prison that was built by his father, many young leaders are symbolically trapped in prisons of religious tradition and leadership philosophy built by their spiritual fathers. I don't know any leader who would intentionally build a prison for the next generation, but it happens all the time.

When King Saul offered his armor to young David, he was sincerely trying to help David fight Goliath. He was not trying to imprison David in an outdated method of warfare. David respectfully declined to wear the armor and employ the methods of the older generation. He preferred a leather sling and smooth stones—a method that was common in his shepherd culture. Saul did not force David to wear his armor. As long as the endgame was killing the giant, Saul was okay with David using his own methods and material.

I wish older leaders would follow Saul's example and not force the next generation to use methods and strategies that worked for us. And I wish more younger leaders would follow David's example and show some respect when they decline methods that they feel are outdated.

So often leaders are sincerely trying to help the next generation when, in reality, they are building prisons made of heavy armor, antique weaponry, and irrelevant religious tradition.

Despite what you may have heard, personal spiritual growth and leadership development is a slow process, not an instant miracle breakthrough. The prophet told Samson's parents that their child would "begin to save Israel" from the oppression of the Philistines (Judges 13:5). Samson was called to *begin a process* of spiritual renewal and national reformation that was to be *finished* by the next generation.

Many of us are too impatient and too short sighted for that. We want to start and finish it all right now. We want— no, we demand—instant answers and miracle maturity. But, that's rarely how God does things. He's more of the multi-generational process kind of God. He's usually not in a hurry.

Doing multi-generational leadership requires patience and perseverance. Multi-generational leadership development that addresses the multiplication challenge and solves the leadership shortage requires laser focus and hard work.

Every leader will either build a platform or a prison for the next generation. Joe Martin was preaching from a platform built by his father, and James Ryle was trapped in a prison built by his father.

Every leader will either build men or monuments. Insecure and arrogant leaders build monuments to themselves. Secure and humble leaders build other leaders. What are you building?

DISCUSSION QUESTIONS X

1. How can insecurity and self-preservation make it diffi-cult to work with talented young leaders?
2. How do you respond to over-honor? How should you respond?
3. How can you empower others to lead with you? What might happen if you do not? What might happen if you do?
4. Are you building a platform or a prison for the next generation? What can you do to build a platform?

AFTERWORD

I grew up in Victory both figuratively and literally. Many of the leaders mentioned in this book were my children's church teachers at one point. My dad, Joey Bonifacio, is the "Discipleship is relationship" guy. The Murrell boys were our best friends growing up.

Because of this, I had a different perspective on these stories. To me, Pastor Ferdie and Pastor Jun weren't the young, inexperienced leaders described here. I knew them as the fiery, passionate preachers who were always inspiring and convicting, and a little scary.

The accounts of how they were empowered to preach very early on are the stuff of legend, and were told to us younger leaders when we were similarly empowered. We tell these stories to the younger leaders coming after us. Many times, the details are a little wrong, but the spirit is the same: an older leader empowers a younger leader by taking a risk on him or her.

In short, the hard work of the generation before us has given birth to an empowering leadership culture. What they worked hard to create, we now enjoy as a natural ambiance. This is the power of culture—if we will build it faithfully, it becomes an invisible, guiding hand.

Pastor Steve has been described as a level-five leader because of a combination of intense will to succeed and genuine humility. Through the work described in this book, he's built a culture where level-five leadership thrives. By genuine humility, I don't mean there isn't any bragging going on. There's a lot of it actually. But it's what they brag about that teaches us what's important.

They brag about being the second man on a team. They brag about the times they've been corrected. They brag about the teams they get to serve with. They brag about how much better their successors are. Most of all, they brag about how so little of the work was from them and how much of it is really from God.

This is the legacy of their generation. And it's an inheritance we, the next generation of leaders, need to preserve for those who are coming after us. This book captures their stories, and we read them so we can repeat them and add our own "to a generation yet unborn," as the psalmist says.

In the beginning of the book, Pastor Steve describes a meeting where Victory faced a problem in our leadership development. I remember that meeting well. Thankfully, with the adjustments made, we are back on track and closing the leadership gap. The problem with this is that it creates more growth, which necessitates more leaders.

If the book started with a leadership crisis, permit me to end it with yet another one. For the past seven years, I have been entrusted to lead our national campus ministry. With an amazing team, we took the current group and grew it from sixty full-time fully funded campus missionaries to 360; from 4,000 students in our meetings to 20,000.

Late 2015, one after the other, our top three national campus ministry leaders were promoted outside of campus ministry. I was happy for them and eager to see them succeed. They also left behind young leaders to take their places.

But I was also nervous. Could we keep growing even without them? Would the new leaders be ready? What if the magic was gone? The pressure to continue growing loomed at the back of my mind.

While I outwardly looked confident, God knew my heart, and He addressed it quickly. While on a mission trip to China, one of our Chinese women leaders said she had a word for me from God:

> I see you running and jumping over many things. Each time the gap gets larger and larger, but you run without fear. You jump with confidence because you know God will carry you across.

> But then I see that you are now approaching the biggest gap yet. And this time, you hesitated. You paused before jumping. God is telling you now to jump again. He carried you over the previous gaps, and He will carry you over now.

> Also, you think you are jumping alone. But look around you. There are many young leaders who will jump with you. Tell them the vision. Let them run with you. Jump together. God will carry you all over.

I heard the humbling reminder: God brings the growth, not me. But there was also the encouragement to empower young leaders. Six months later, our new team has proven themselves several times over and I couldn't be more excited for the future.

In the same way, I pray that you have a huge mission from God. I pray that it's so big that it causes you to pause and wonder if you'll make it. At that point, I pray that you will still jump with confidence knowing that as you trust God, lead with a team, and train new leaders, you'll make it.

—JOSEPH BONIFACIO
Every Nation Campus
Asia Director

ACKNOWLEDGMENTS

Special thanks to the following people who made this book possible:

Rachel Murrell, overall project director and Chicago Manual of Style guru.

Jordan Murphy, project manager and guitar aficionado.

Sam Barker, cover design and St Louis Cardinals fanatic.

Paul Uson, cover design and Real LIFE Foundation alumnus.

Don Luna, layout artist and drummer.

Gizelle Pangilinan, graphic designer and contemporary ballet dancer.

Varsha Daswani, copy editor extraordinaire and Victory historian.

Esther Suson, editorial assistant to Varsha and martial arts enthusiast.

Gigi Landicho, Manila office traffic director and guardian of the schedule.

Carlos Antonio, Every Nation global communications team leader and Gary V impersonator.

Jay Abola, Every Nation Philippines communications team leader and Carlos Antonio impersonator.

ABOUT THE AUTHORS

Steve Murrell is the cofounder and president of Every Nation Churches & Ministries, a church planting movement with a vision to plant churches and campus ministries in every nation. So far, Every Nation has planted churches in seventy-three countries.

In 1984, Steve and his wife, Deborah, went to the Philippines for a thirty-day mission trip that turned into thirty years and counting. They are the founding pastors of Victory Manila, one church that meets in twenty-five congregations across Metro Manila and has planted churches in over seventy Philippine cities and twenty-two nations. Today, Victory has more than 10,000 discipleship-group leaders and interns that meet in coffee shops, offices, campuses, and homes throughout Metro Manila.

Steve is the author of *WikiChurch, 100 Years From Now,* and *My First, Second, & Third Attempts at Parenting,* and coauthor of *The Purple Book,* a foundational Bible study with more than one million copies in print.

Steve serves on the board of the Real LIFE Foundation, a Christian nonprofit that seeks to provide underprivileged Filipino youth with a better future by transforming their communities and giving them access to a good education.

After living in the Philippines for twenty-four years, Steve and Deborah now split their time between Manila and Nashville. They have three adult sons who were born and raised in Manila and now live in the United States.

For more information, blogs, social media, and podcasts, visit stevemurrell.com.

William Murrell is a PhD candidate in History at Vanderbilt University in Nashville, Tennessee. His research focuses on Muslim-Christian relations in Syria during the Crusades.

William grew up in the Philippines and attended Victory Manila for the first eighteen years of his life. During that time, he attended many of the Victory discipleship groups that meet in coffee shops, offices, campuses, and homes throughout Metro Manila, where they often went through materials such as *The Purple Book*.

After living in the Philippines for eighteen years, William moved to the United States, where he attended Lipscomb University. He then spent a year teaching English in Bernay, France, and a year in Oxford, England, where he earned a masters degree in Medieval History. He also spent a summer in Jordan studying Arabic.

William and his wife, Rachel, have two young children and live in Nashville, Tennessee.

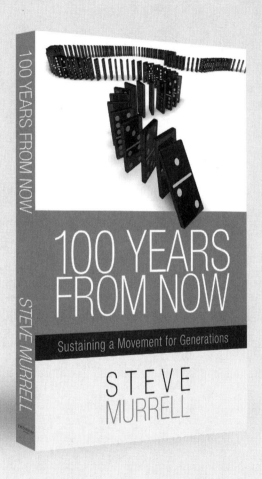
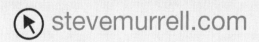

HAVE YOU DONE THE **PURPLE BOOK**?

MAKE A DECISION THAT LASTS FOREVER

THE **PURPLE** BOOK

Biblical Foundations for Building Strong Disciples

RICE BROOCKS
STEVE MURRELL

ZONDERVAN

☑ Develop solid biblical foundations.

☑ Grow strong in your Christian life.

☑ Stand firm in God's Word.

EVERY NATION
PRODUCTIONS

To order copies of The Purple Book, email orders@everynation.org.ph.

Plenty of parenting books focus on how to fix bad behavior, but *My First, Second & Third Attempts at Parenting* deals with the heart

STEVE MURRELL

MY FIRST, SECOND & THIRD ATTEMPTS AT PARENTING

Discovering the Heart of Parenting

DISCOVER THE MOST IMPORTANT PAR OF PARENTING

GET YOUR COPY TODAY!

Available at amazon